Kutless
Hearts of the Innocent

Music transcriptions by Pete Billmann and David Stocker

ISBN-13: 978-1-4234-1973-1
ISBN-10: 1-4234-1973-1

HAL•LEONARD®
CORPORATION

7777 W. BLUEMOUND RD. P.O. BOX 13819 MILWAUKEE, WI 53213

Visit Hal Leonard Online at
www.halleonard.com

Hearts of the Innocent

Words and Music by Jon Micah Sumrall, Aaron Sprinkle and Ryan Shrout

Drop D tuning, down 1/2 step:
(low to high) Db-Ab-Db-Gb-Bb-Eb

Intro

Moderately slow ♩ = 90

*Gtr. 1 (dist.)

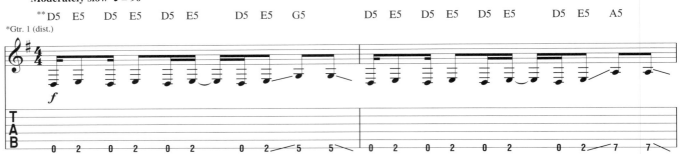

*Doubled throughout

**Chord symbols reflect implied harmony.

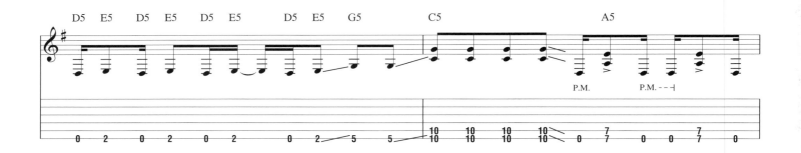

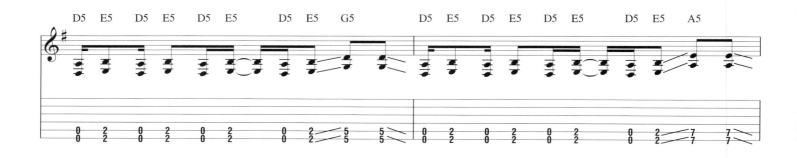

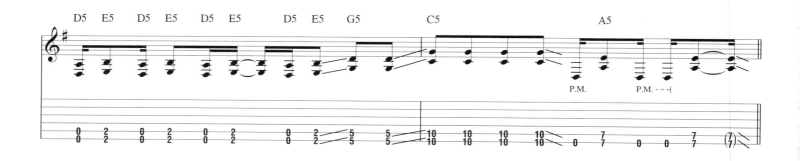

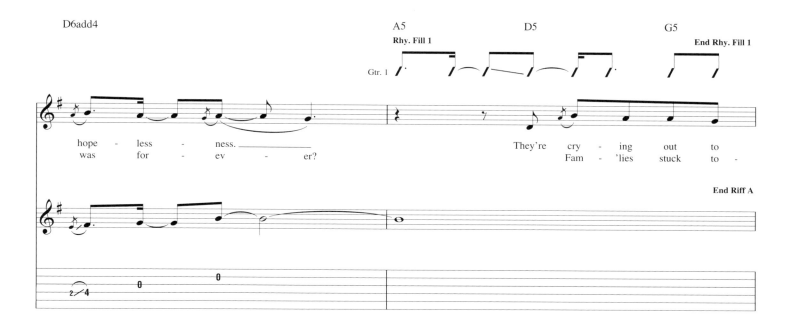

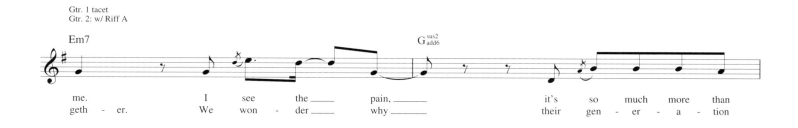

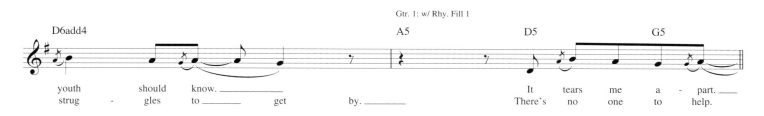

3

of the in - no - cent? We're teach - ing them to

End Riff B

End Rhy. Fig. 1

Gtr. 1: w/ Rhy. Fig. 1 (1 1/2 times)
Gtr. 3: w/ Riff B (1 1/2 times)

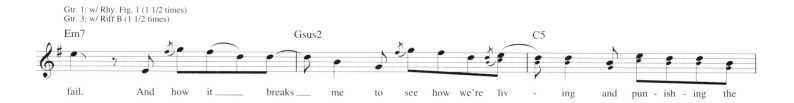

fail. And how it _____ breaks _____ me to see how we're liv - ing and pun - ish - ing the

ones that need us to care. _____ To see them hurt - ing feels like

To Coda ⊕

Interlude

Gtr. 3 tacet

knuck - les to the back of my head. _____

Gtr. 3

Gtr. 1

P.M.   P.M. - ┤   P.M.

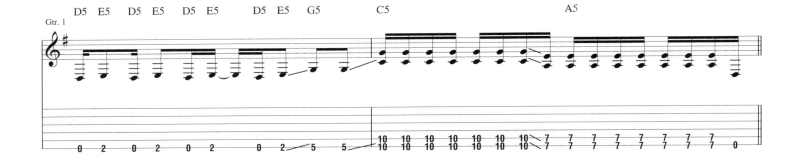

Guitar Solo

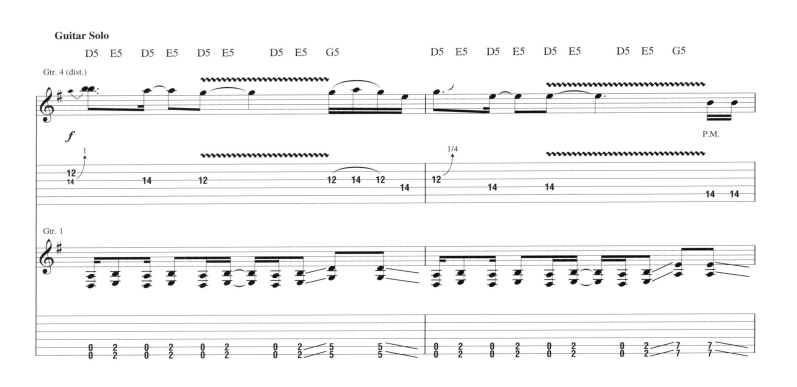

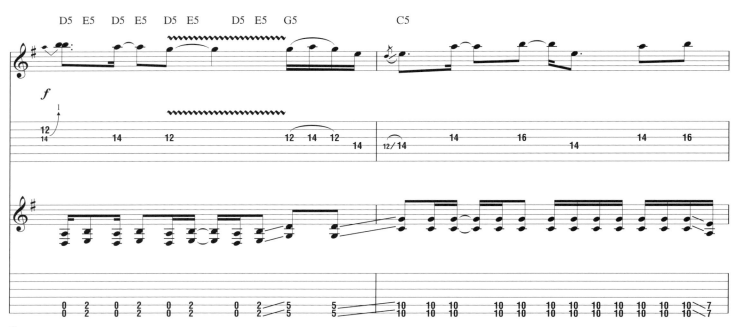

Shut Me Out

Words and Music by Jon Micah Sumrall and Ethan Luck

Drop D tuning, down 1/2 step:
(low to high) Db-Ab-Db-Gb-Bb-Eb

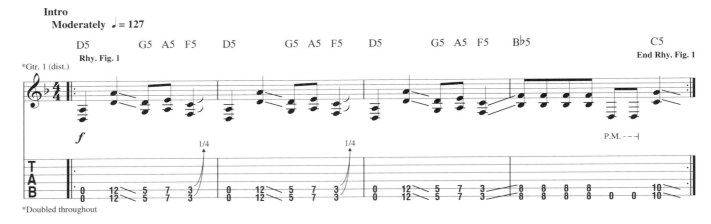

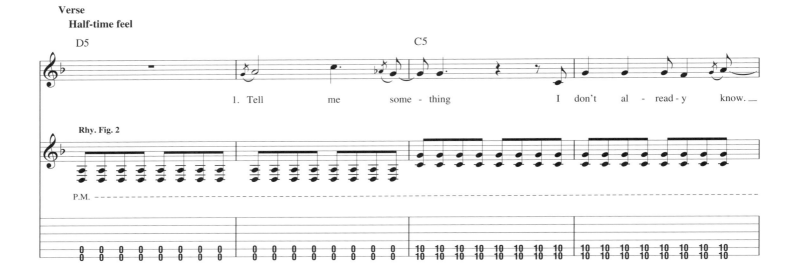

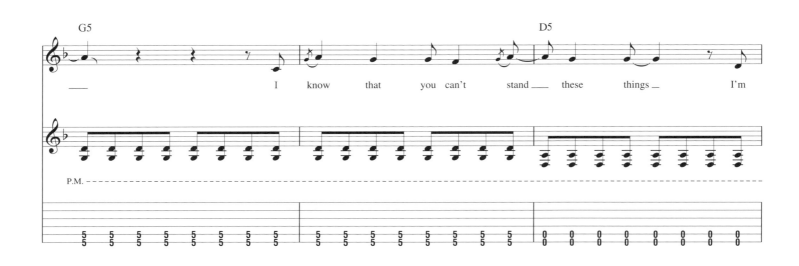

Gtr. 1: w/ Rhy. Fig. 2 (1st 6 meas.)

preach-ing in ___ the streets. ___ But how can I con-tain ___ the

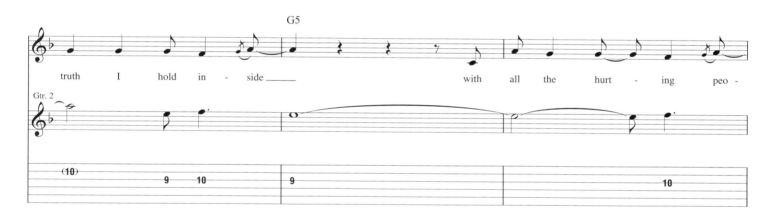

truth I hold in-side ___ with all the hurt - ing peo-

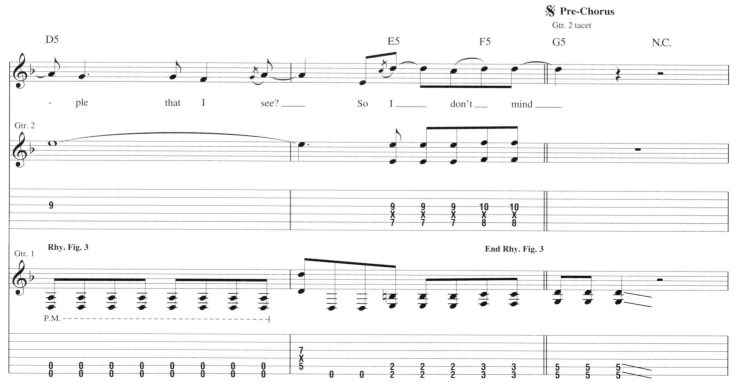

- ple that I see? ___ So I ___ don't mind ___

Pre-Chorus

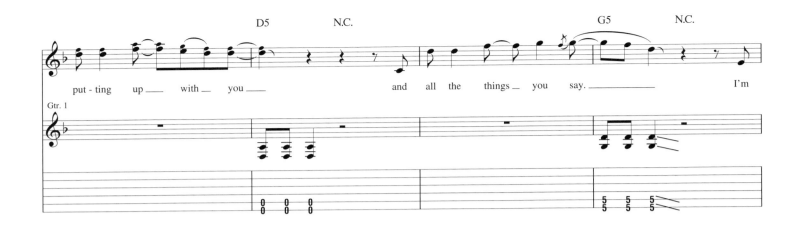

put - ting up __ with __ you __ and all the things __ you say. _____ I'm

Gtr. 1

End half-time feel

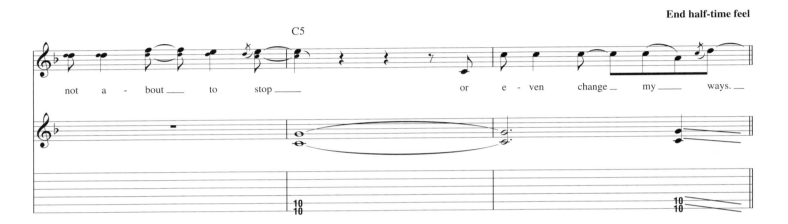

not a - bout __ to stop __ or e - ven change __ my __ ways. __

Chorus

1st time, Gtr. 1: w/ Rhy. Fig. 1 (2 times)
2nd time, Gtr. 1: w/ Rhy. Fig. 1 (1 1/2 times)

__ There's noth - ing __ you __ can say __ that will take __ me a - way __ from this life. __

To Coda ⊕

__ There's noth - ing __ you __ can do ___ to shut me up __ when I'm speak - in' the truth.

Verse
Half-time feel

Gtr. 1: w/ Rhy. Fig. 2 (1 3/4 times)

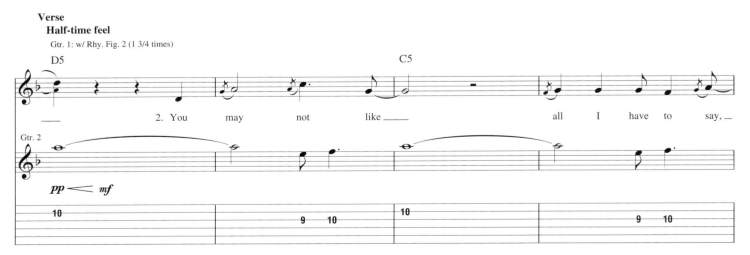

__ 2. You may not like ____ all I have to say, __

Gtr. 2

pp < mf

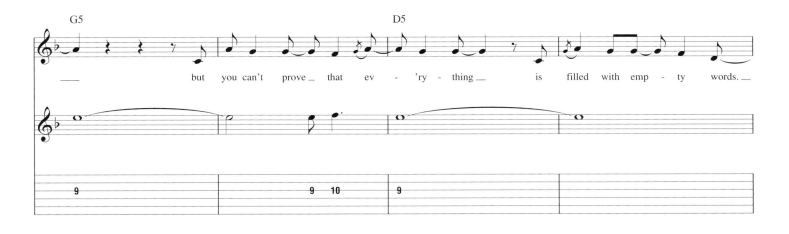

but you can't prove _ that ev - 'ry - thing _ is filled with emp - ty words. _

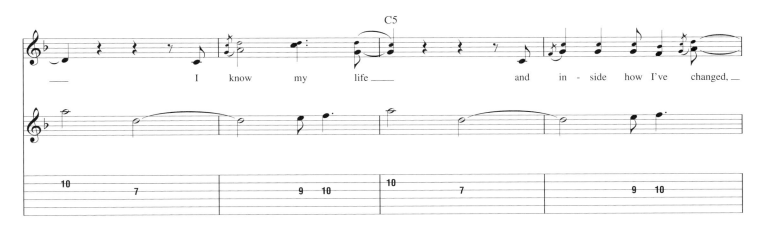

I know my life _ and in - side how I've changed, _

D.S. al Coda

Gtr. 1: w/ Rhy. Fig. 3

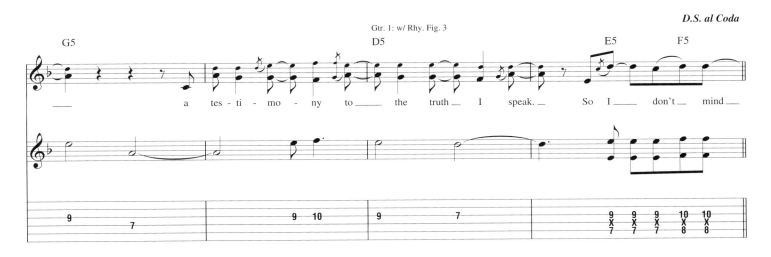

a tes - ti - mo - ny to _ the truth _ I speak. _ So I _ don't _ mind _

Coda

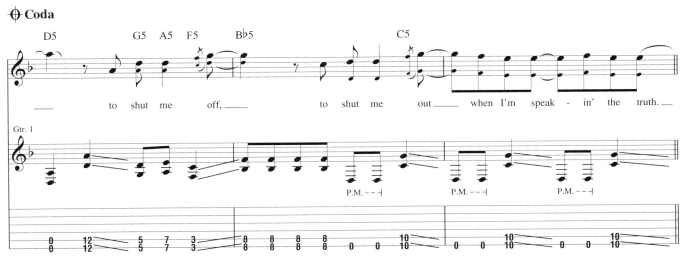

to shut me off, _ to shut me out _ when I'm speak - in' the truth. _

Gtr. 1

Guitar Solo

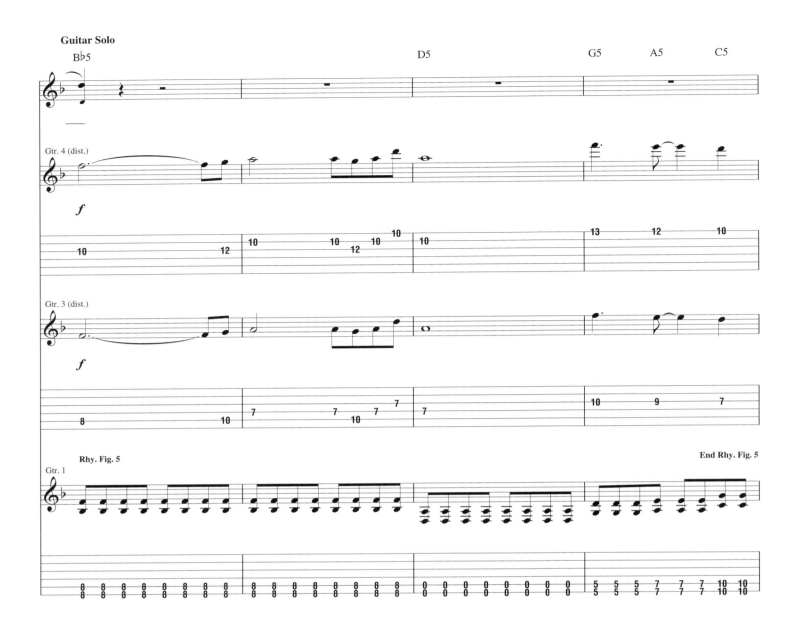

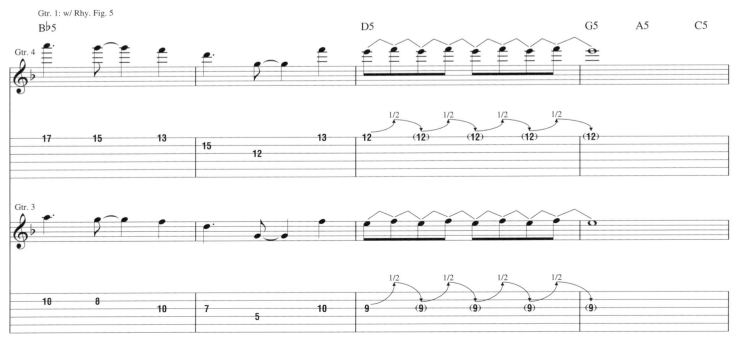

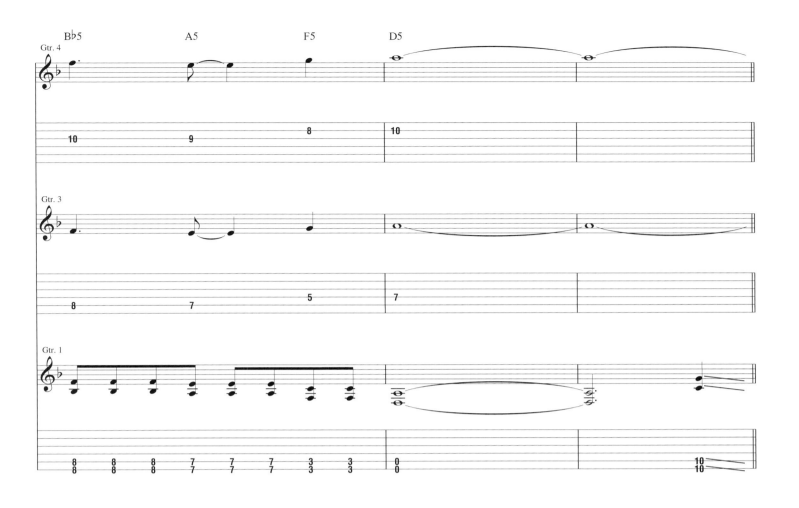

Chorus

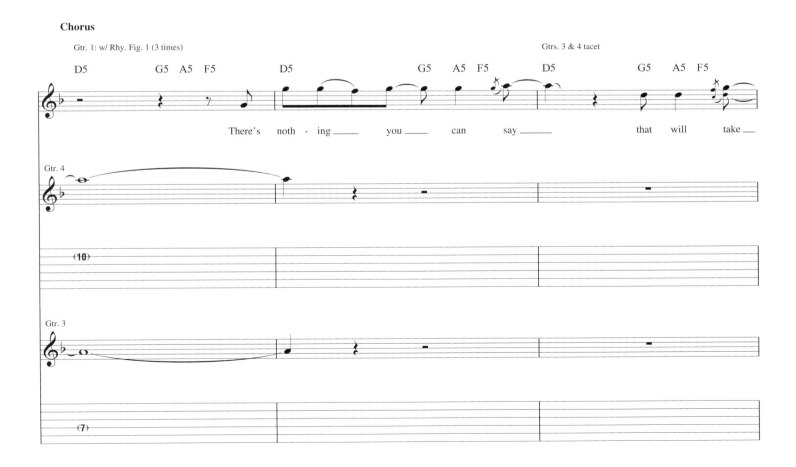

There's noth - ing ____ you ____ can say ____ that will take ____

me a -way from this life. There's noth - ing you can do

to shut me up when I'm speak - in' the truth. There's

noth - ing you can say that will take me a -way from this life.

There's noth - ing you can do to shut me off,

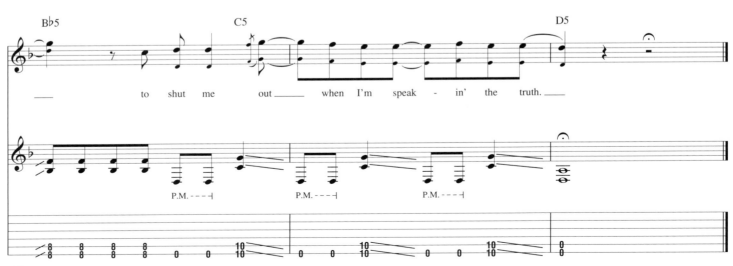

to shut me out when I'm speak - in' the truth.

Beyond the Surface

Words and Music by Jon Micah Sumrall, Aaron Sprinkle and James Mead

Drop D tuning, down 1/2 step:
(low to high) Db-Ab-Db-Gb-Bb-Eb

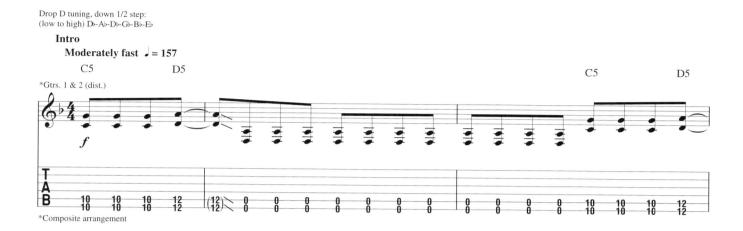

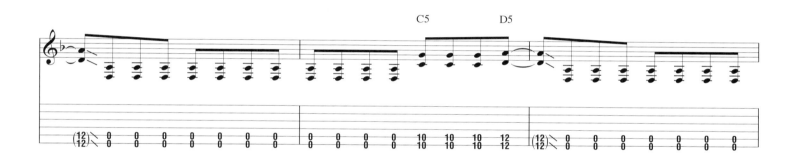

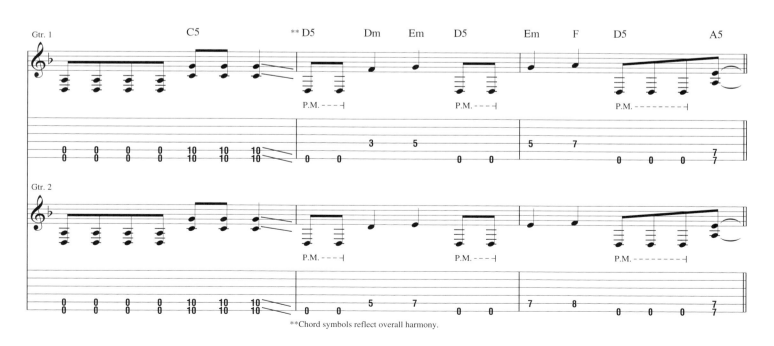

*Chord symbols reflect overall harmony.

Pre-Chorus

that push _____ me a - way _____
and push _____ you a - way _____

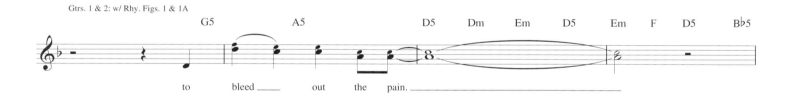

to bleed _____ out the pain. _____

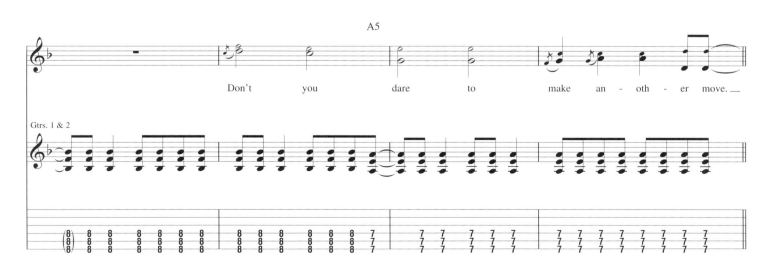

Don't you dare to make an - oth - er move. ___

Chorus

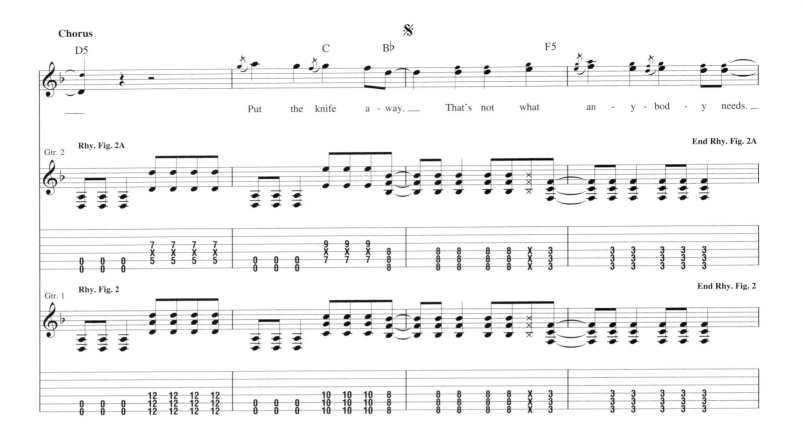

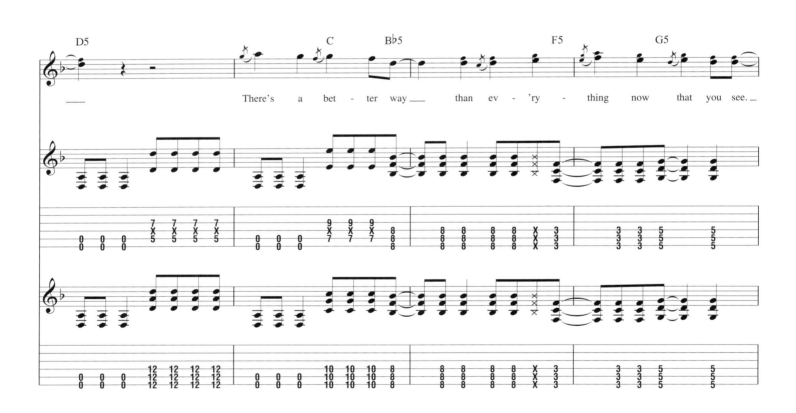

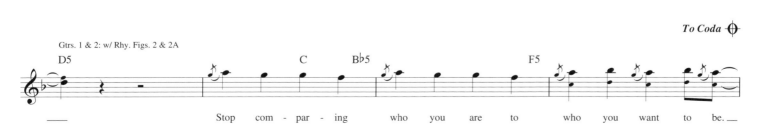

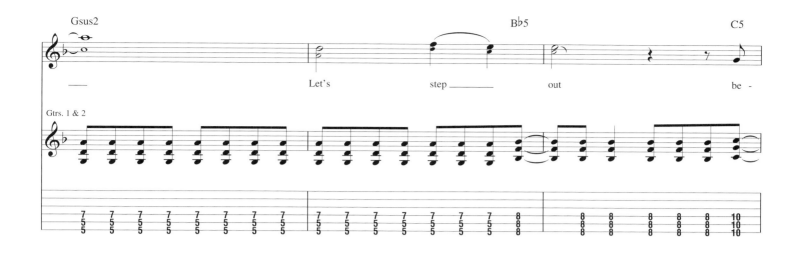

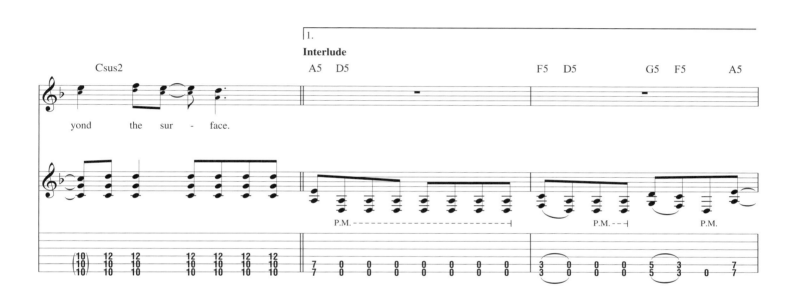

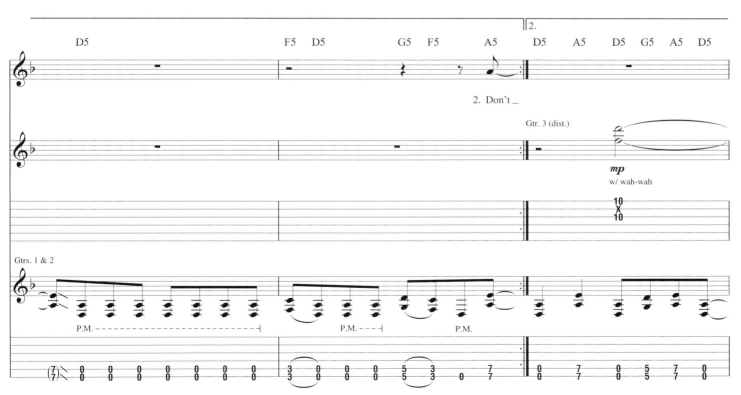

Guitar Solo

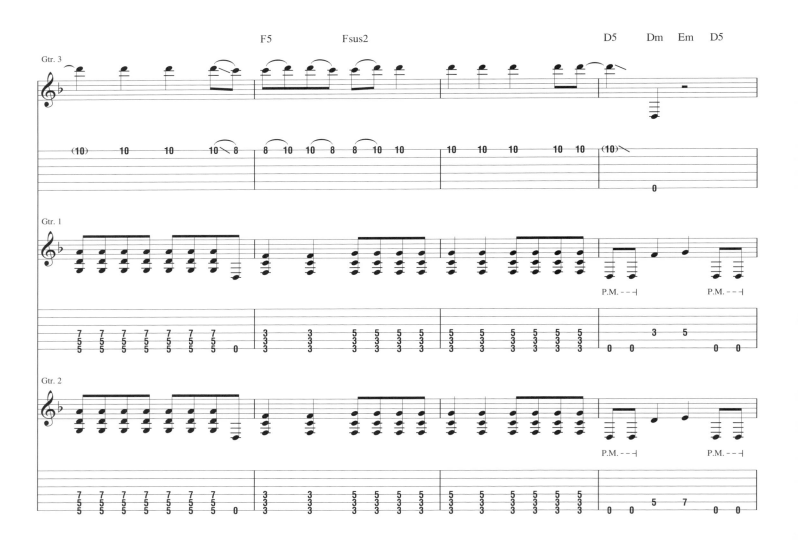

Smile

Words and Music by Jon Micah Sumrall and Aaron Sprinkle

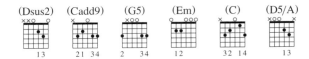

Gtrs. 1, 3 & 4: Tune down 1/2 step, Capo V:
(low to high) E♭-A♭-D♭-G♭-B♭-E♭
Gtrs. 2, 5 & 6: Tune down 1/2 step:
(low to high) E♭-A♭-D♭-G♭-B♭-E♭

Intro
Slowly ♩ = 76

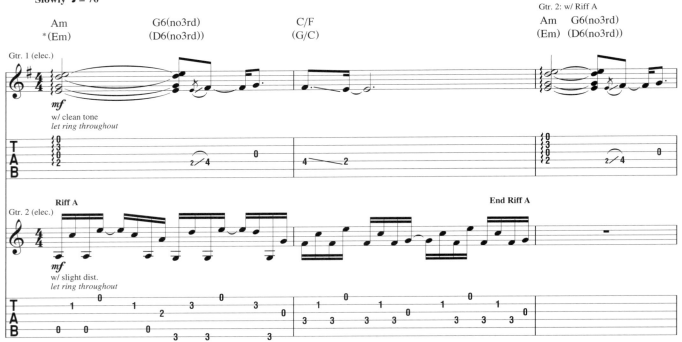

*Symbols in parentheses represent chord names respective to capoed guitar.
Symbols above reflect actual sounding chord. Capoed fret is "0" in tab.
Chord symbols reflect implied harmony.

Verse

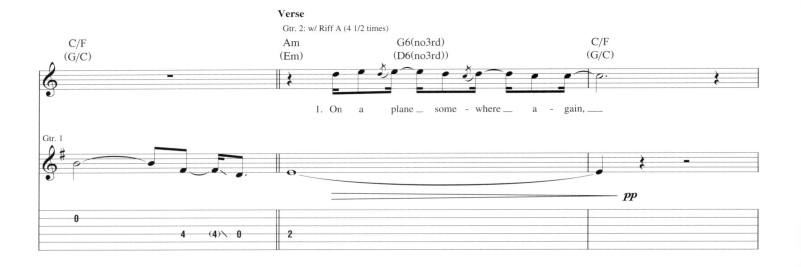

I slide in-to my win-dow seat. She was sit-ting there,

one seat o-ver, so I said, "Hel-lo. How are you to-day?"

𝄋 Pre-Chorus

With my smile I could see the
I can see the

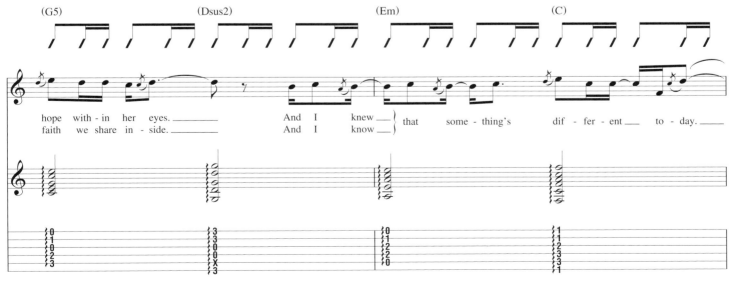

hope with-in her eyes. And I knew } that some-thing's dif-fer-ent to-day.
faith we share in-side. And I know }

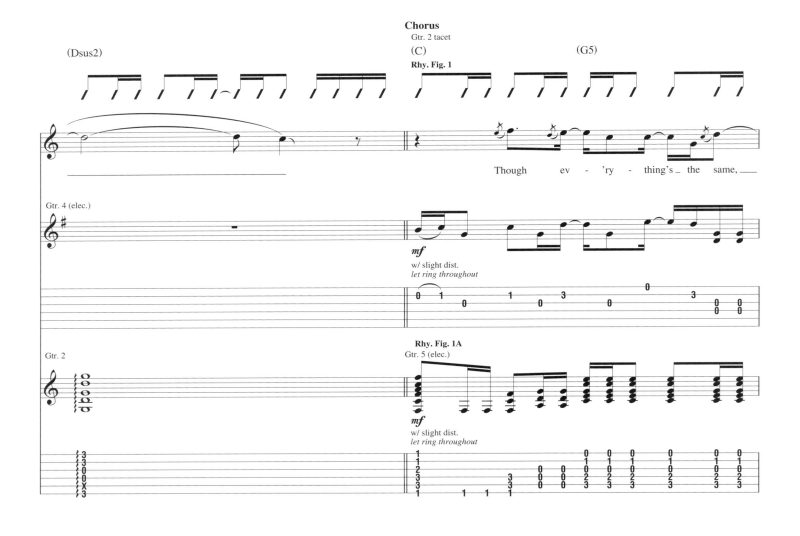

Chorus

Gtr. 2 tacet

Though ev - 'ry - thing's the same,

in - side there's some - thing real, a faith which caus - es me to change.

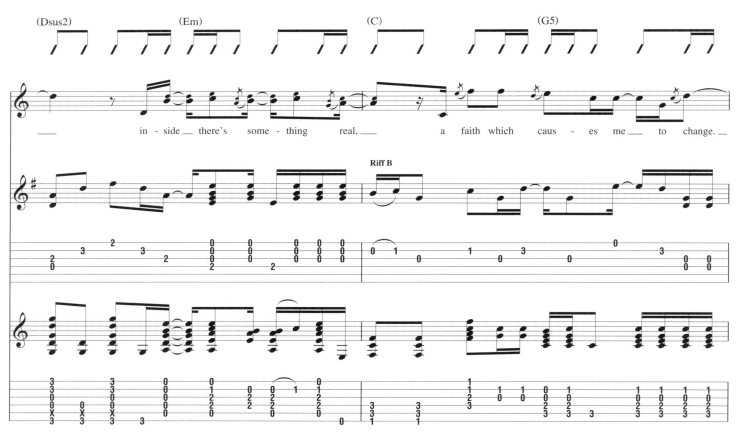

(What's dif-f'rent now?) _____

A spark is gleam-ing in my eye, _____

like di-'mond stars that fill the sky. _____ I think a smile says it all, _____

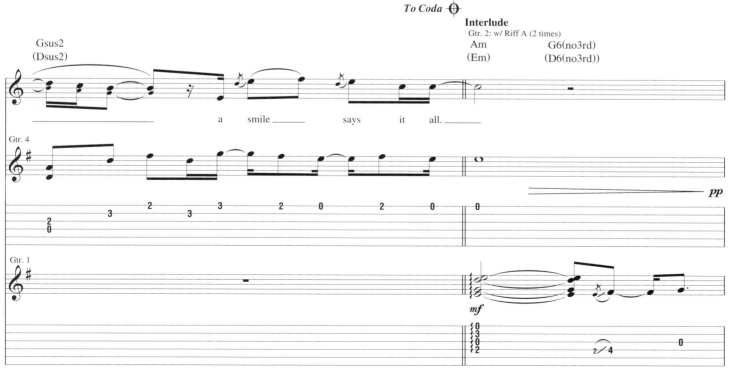

a smile _____ says it all. _____

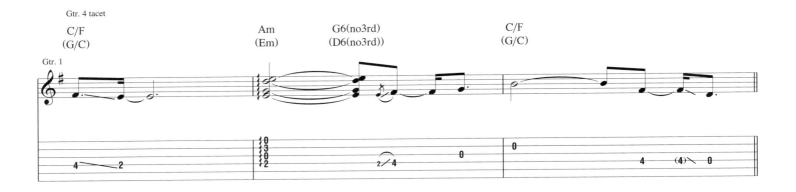

Verse

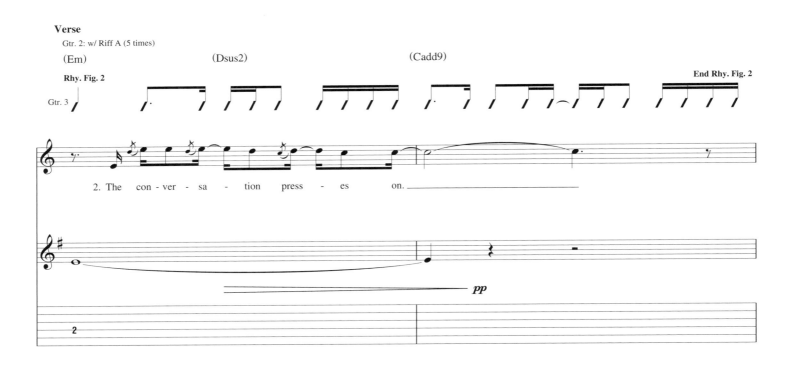

2. The con-ver-sa-tion press-es on.

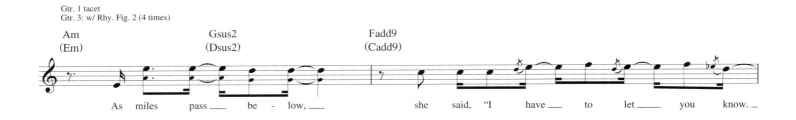

As miles pass ___ be-low, ___ she said, "I have ___ to let ___ you know. ___

___ You seem so dif-fer-ent ___ to me." ___

There is a joy ___ in - side. The love of God ___ is all ___ I know ___

D.S. al Coda

___ from which this could o - rig - i - nate. _____ With one smile ___

⊕ Coda

Gtrs. 3 & 5: w/ Rhy. Figs. 1 & 1A (last 2 meas., 2 times)

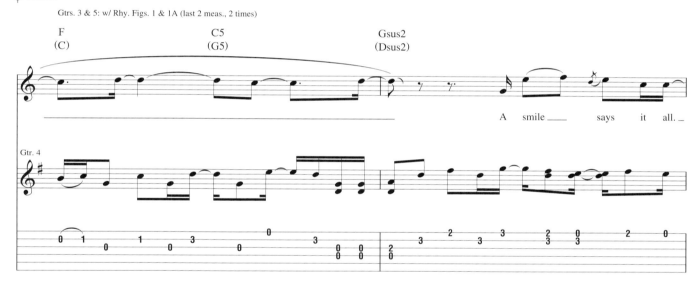

A smile ___ says it all. ___

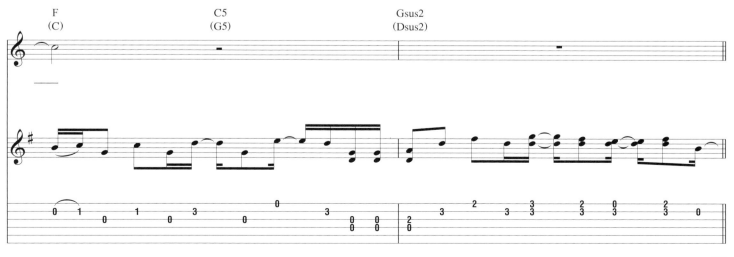

Bridge

Gtr. 2: w/ Riff C (2 times)
Gtr. 4 tacet
Gtr. 5: w/ Rhy. Fig. 3 (2 times)

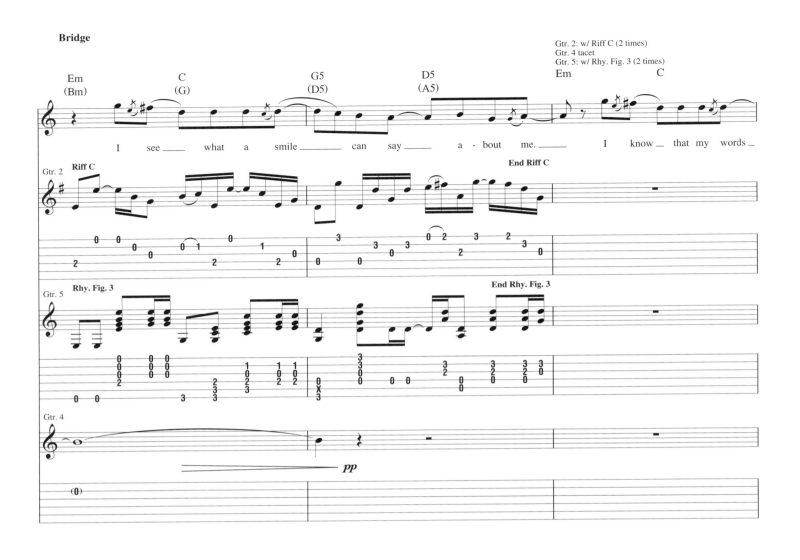

I see ___ what a smile ___ can say ___ a - bout me. ___ I know ___ that my words ___

___ are not al - ways what speak. ___ Some - times ___ it's not ___ what I say ___ that the world ___

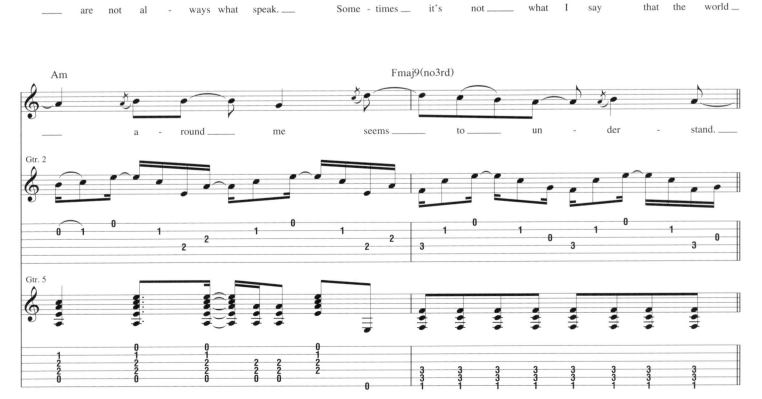

___ a - round ___ me seems ___ to ___ un - der - stand.

Outro

Gtrs. 3 & 5: w/ Rhy. Figs. 1 & 1A (last 2 meas., 2 1/2 times)
Gtr. 4: w/ Riff B (2 1/2 times)
Gtr. 6 tacet

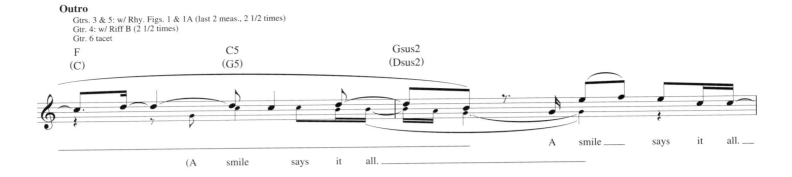

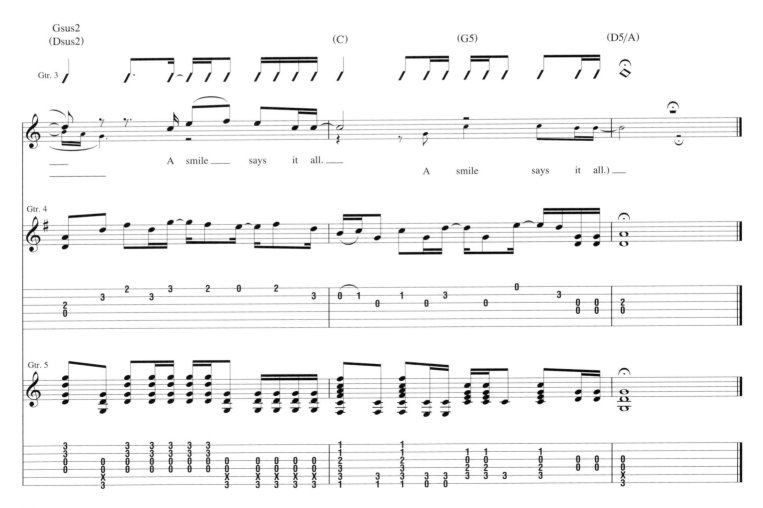

Promise of a Lifetime

Words and Music by Jon Micah Sumrall and Aaron Sprinkle

Gtrs. 2, 3 & 5: Capo II

Intro

Slowly ♩ = 70

*Piano arr. for gtr.

**Chord symbols reflect basic harmony.

1. I have fal - len _____ to my knees _____

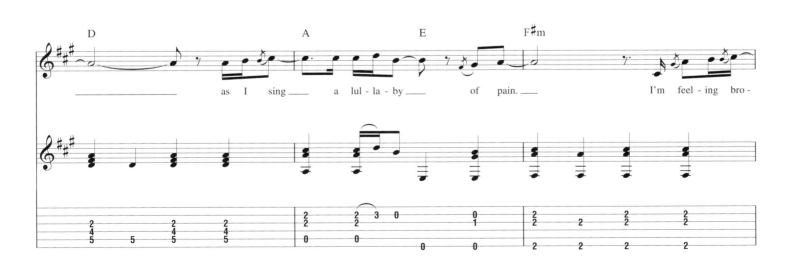

_____ as I sing _____ a lul - la - by _____ of pain. _____ I'm feel - ing bro -

E   D   A   E

-ken   in my mel - o - dy   as I sing   to help the tears   go a - way.

Dadd9   E
*(Cadd9)   (D)

Then I re - mem - ber   the pledge You made   to me.

**Gtr. 2 (acous.)

mp
let ring throughout

**Doubled throughout

Gtr. 1

Symbols in parentheses represent chord names respective to capoed guitar.
Symbols above reflect actual sounding chords. Capoed fret is "0" in tab.

𝄋 Chorus

1st time, Gtr. 1 tacet
2nd time, Gtr. 5 tacet

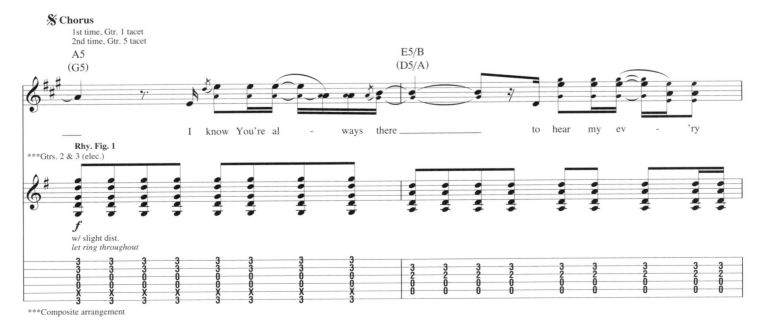

A5   E5/B
(G5)   (D5/A)

I know You're al - ways there   to hear my ev - 'ry

Rhy. Fig. 1
***Gtrs. 2 & 3 (elec.)

f
w/ slight dist.
let ring throughout

***Composite arrangement

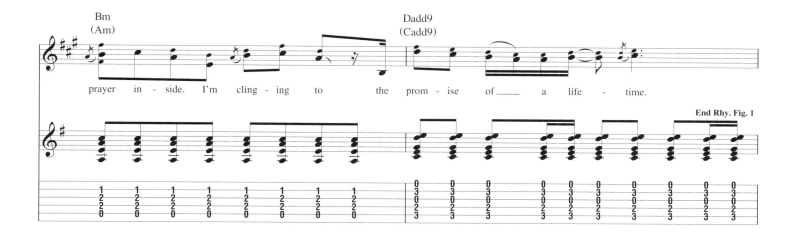

prayer in - side. I'm cling - ing to the prom - ise of ___ a life - time.

End Rhy. Fig. 1

Gtrs. 2 & 3: w/ Rhy. Fig. 1

I hear the words ___ You say, ___ to nev - er walk ___ a -

To Coda ⊕

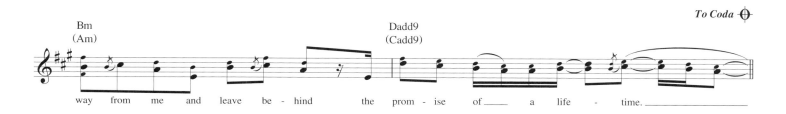

way from me and leave be - hind the prom - ise of ___ a life - time. ___

Interlude

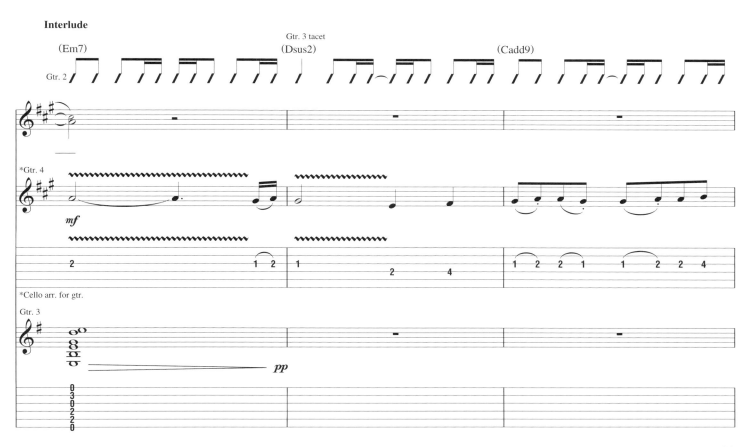

33

Verse

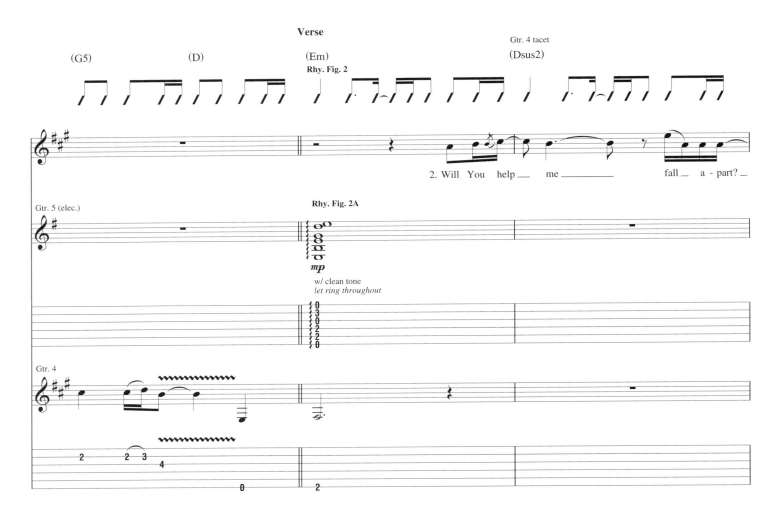

Gtr. 4 tacet

2. Will You help ___ me ___ fall ___ a-part? ___

Gtr. 5 (elec.)

Rhy. Fig. 2A

mp

w/ clean tone
let ring throughout

Gtr. 4

Gtrs. 2 & 5: w/ Rhy. Figs. 2 & 2A

End Rhy. Fig. 2

Pick me   up, ___   and take me   in ___   Your arms. ___   Uh, find my way ___

End Rhy. Fig. 2A

Gtr. 5

Esus2   Dadd9   A5   Esus2
(Dsus2)   (Cadd9)   (G5)   (Dsus2)

___ back   from ___ the   storm, ___   and You show ___   me how to   grow ___   through the   change. ___

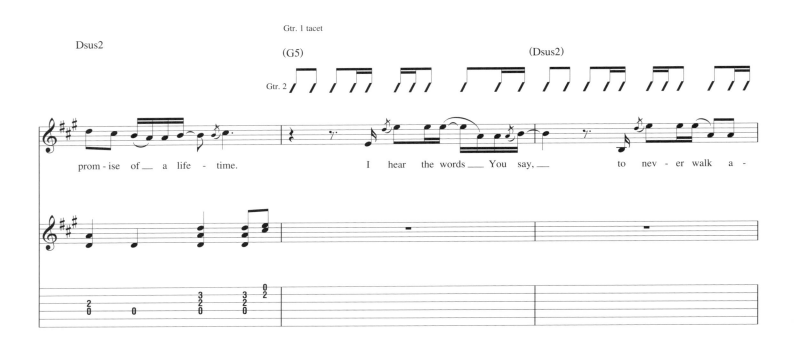

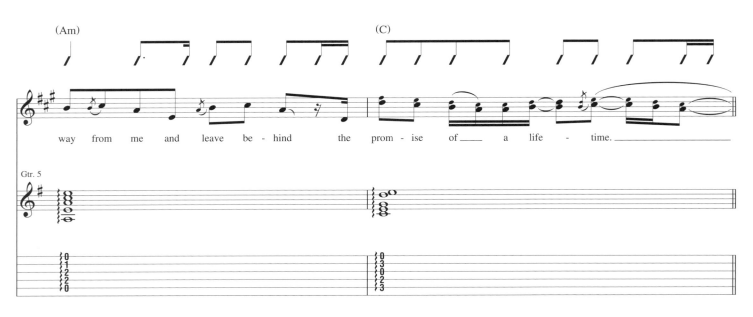

Outro-Chorus

Gtrs. 2 & 3: w/ Rhy. Fig. 1 (1 1/2 times)
Gtr. 5 tacet

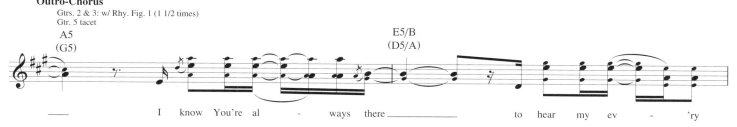

I know You're al - ways there ___ to hear my ev - 'ry

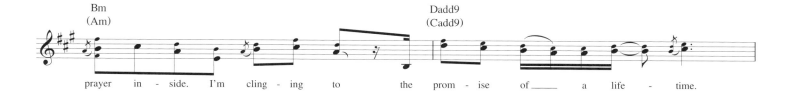

prayer in - side. I'm cling - ing to the prom - ise of ___ a life - time.

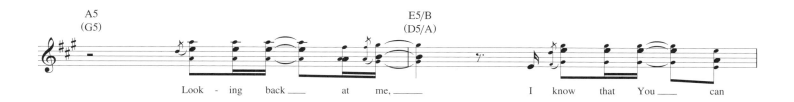

Look - ing back ___ at me, ___ I know that You ___ can

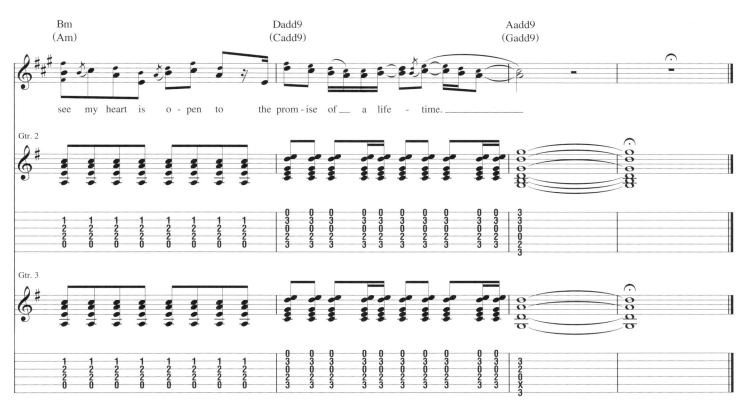

see my heart is o - pen to the prom - ise of ___ a life - time. ___

Winds of Change

Words and Music by Jon Micah Sumrall and Aaron Sprinkle

Drop D tuning, down 1/2 step:
(low to high) Db-Ab-Db-Gb-Bb-Eb

Intro
Moderately slow ♩ = 97

*Chord symbols reflect implied harmony.

Verse
Gtr. 1: w/ Riff A (3 times)

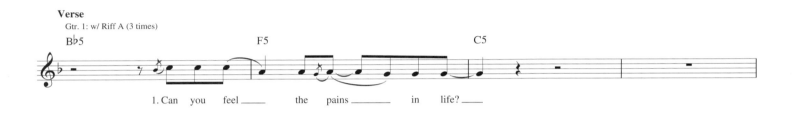

1. Can you feel ___ the pains ___ in life? ___

Wrapped a-round ___ you like ___ they're chains, ___ re-strict-ing all ___ your dreams. ___

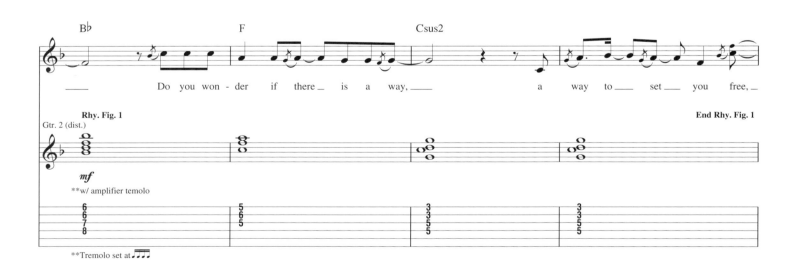

___ Do you won-der if there ___ is a way, ___ a way to ___ set ___ you free, ___

Rhy. Fig. 1
Gtr. 2 (dist.)

End Rhy. Fig. 1

**w/ amplifier temolo

**Tremolo set at

Interlude

Gtr. 1: w/ Riff A

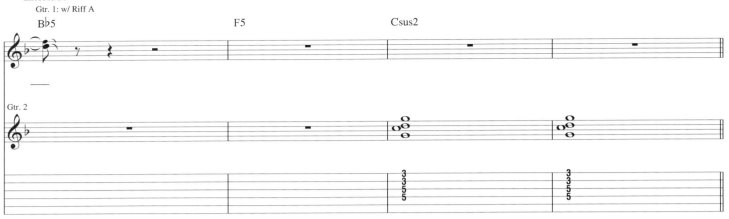

Verse

Gtr. 1: w/ Riff A (3 times)
Gtr. 2: w/ Rhy. Fig. 1 (3 times)

2. Do you feel ____ the winds ____ of change? ____

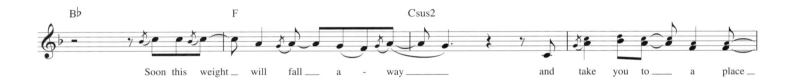

Soon this weight ____ will fall ____ a - way ____ and take you to ____ a place ____

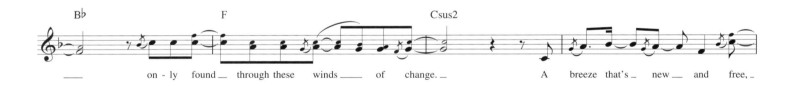

____ on - ly found ____ through these winds ____ of change. ____ A breeze that's ____ new ____ and free, ____

D.S. al Coda

Gtr. 1: w/ Riff B
Gtr. 2: w/ Rhy. Fig. 2

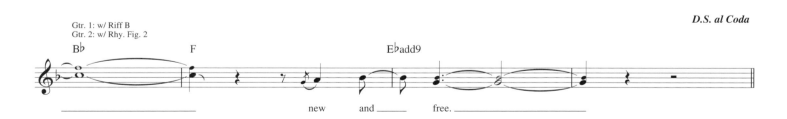

_____ new and ____ free. _____

⊕ Coda

Gtr. 3: w/ Rhy. Fig. 3 (1 3/4 times)

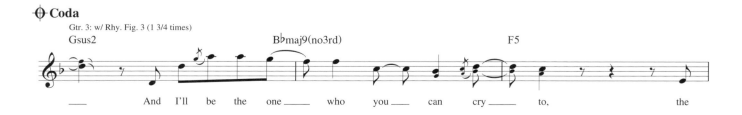

____ And I'll be the one ____ who you ____ can cry ____ to, the

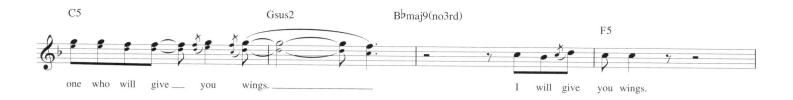

one who will give __ you wings. _____

I will give __ you wings.

Bridge

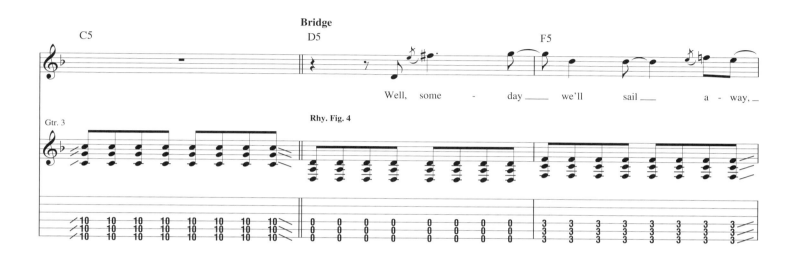

Well, some - day __ we'll sail __ a - way, __

Gtr. 3

Rhy. Fig. 4

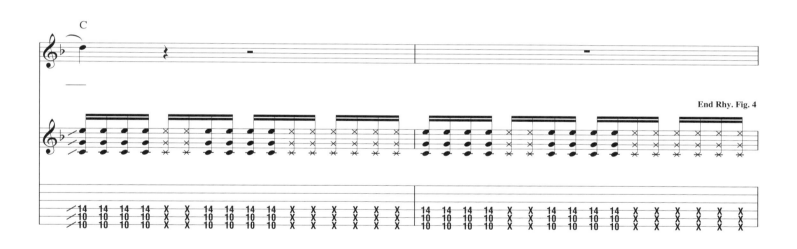

End Rhy. Fig. 4

Gtr. 3: w/ Rhy. Fig. 4 (2 times)

mount - ed up __ on wings __ like ea - gles. __

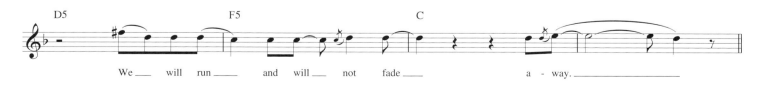

We __ will run __ and will __ not fade __ a - way. _____

Outro-Chorus

So tell me all your dreams, ___ and tell me all your fears, ___ and what ___ you're long -

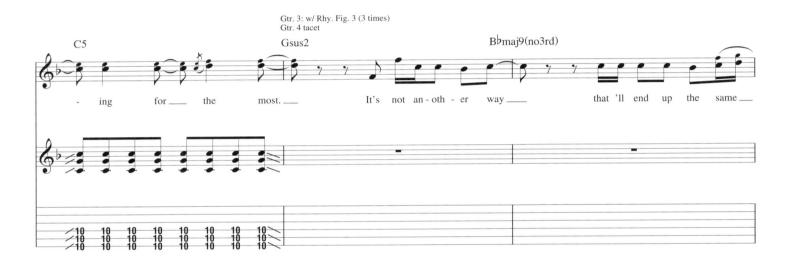

- ing for ___ the most. ___ It's not an - oth - er way ___ that 'll end up the same ___

___ for ___ it's un - der my ___ con - trol. ___ And I'll be the one ___

___ who you ___ can cry ___ to, the one who will give ___ you wings. ___

___ I'll ___ give you wings, the one that will give ___ you wings.

Somewhere in the Sky

Words and Music by Jon Micah Sumrall and James Mead

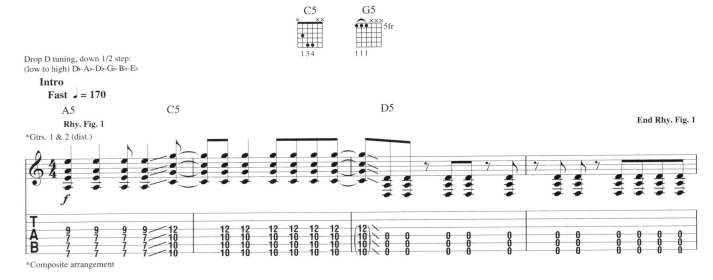

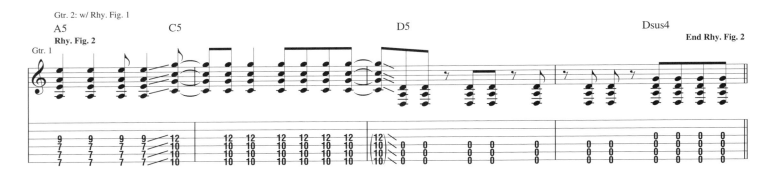

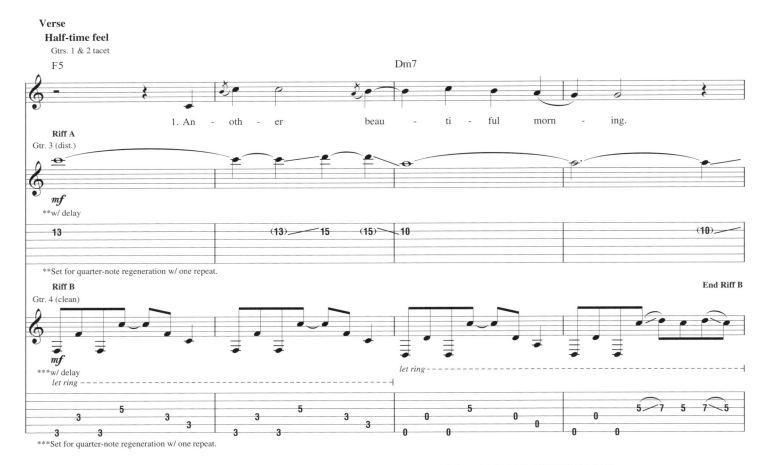

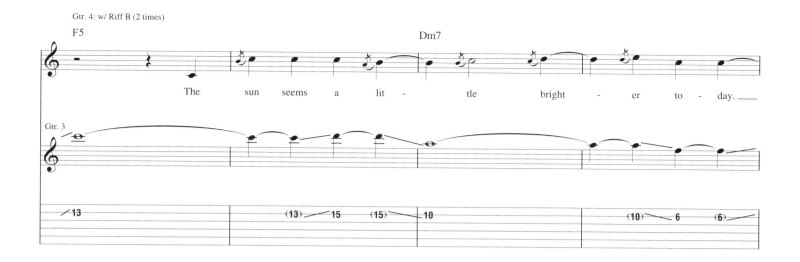

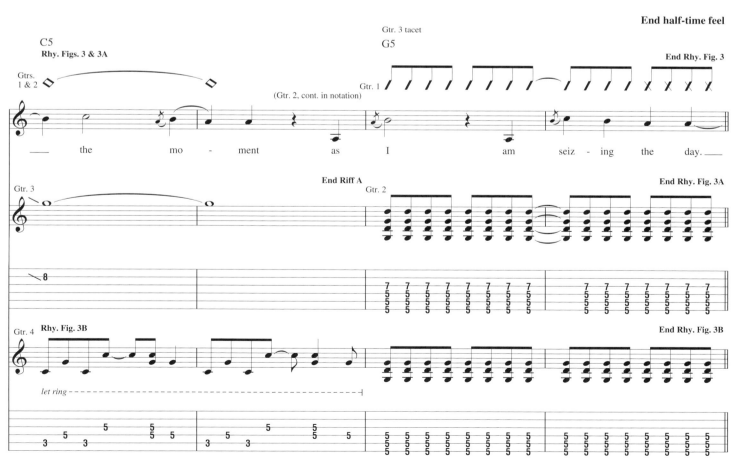

%· Chorus

Gtr. 1: w/ Rhy. Fig. 1
Gtr. 2: w/ Rhy. Fig. 1 (2 times)
Gtr. 4 tacet

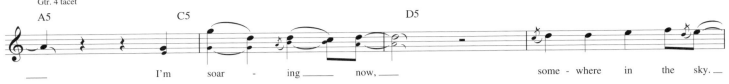

I'm soar - ing ___ now, ___ some - where in the sky. ___

Gtr. 1: w/ Rhy. Fig. 2

The rush ___ of ___ air, ___ nev - er want - ing to ___ come ___

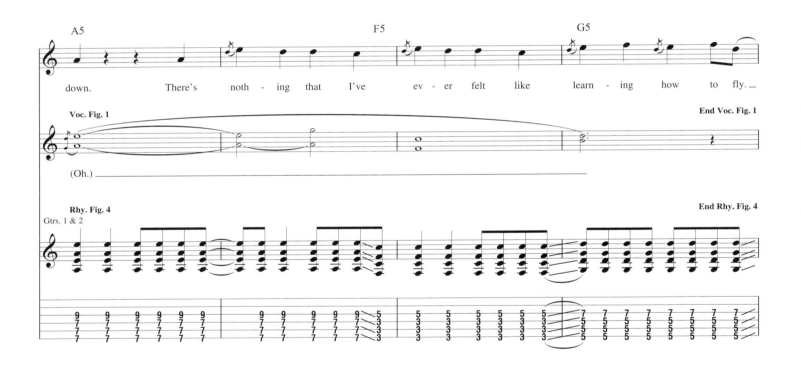

down. There's noth - ing that I've ev - er felt like learn - ing how to fly. ___

Voc. Fig. 1   End Voc. Fig. 1

(Oh.) ___

Rhy. Fig. 4   End Rhy. Fig. 4
Gtrs. 1 & 2

To Coda ⊕

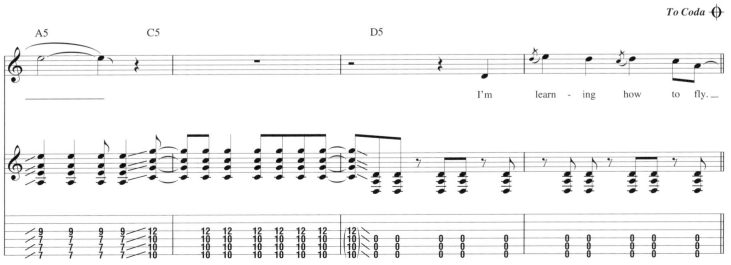

I'm learn - ing how to fly. ___

Half-time feel

Gtrs. 1 & 2 tacet
Gtr. 3: w/ Riff A
Gtr. 4: w/ Riff B (3 times)

2. The free - dom to be _____ in the mo - ment.

The rea - son for mak - ing a mem - o - ry. _____

And nev - er _____ wast - ing _____ all _____ that comes _____

D.S. al Coda
End half-time feel

Gtrs. 1, 2 & 4: w/ Rhy. Figs. 3, 3A & 3B

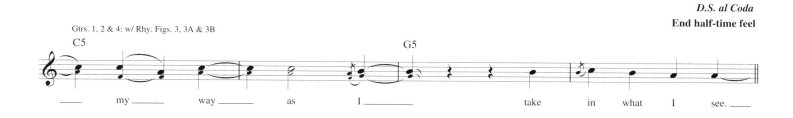

_____ my _____ way _____ as I _____ take in what I see. _____

✛ **Coda**

Bridge

Half-time feel

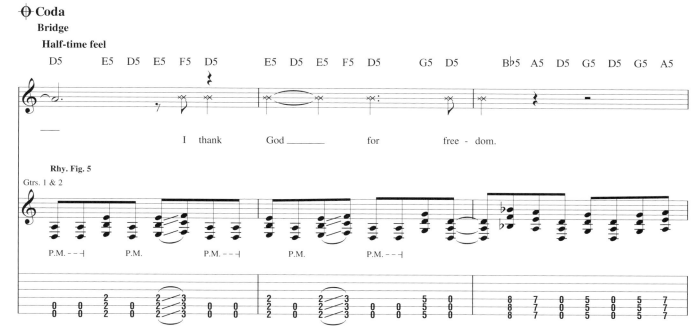

I thank God _____ for free - dom.

Rhy. Fig. 5

Gtrs. 1 & 2

P.M. P.M. P.M. P.M. P.M.

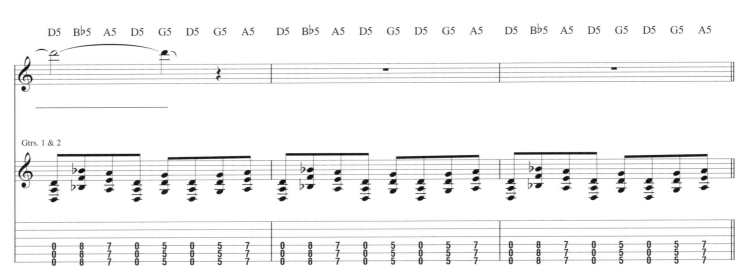

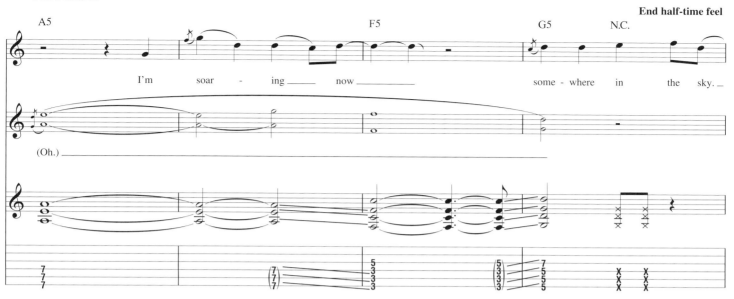

I'm soar - ing _____ now _____ some - where in the sky. _____

(Oh.) _____

Gtr. 1: w/ Rhy. Fig. 1
Gtr. 2: w/ Rhy. Fig. 2

_____ The rush _____ of _____ air, _____ nev - er want - ing to _____ come _____

Bkgd. Voc.: w/ Voc. Fig. 1
Gtrs. 1 & 2: w/ Rhy. Fig. 4

down. There's noth - ing that I've ev - er felt like learn - ing how to fly. _____

Gtrs. 1 & 2: w/ Rhy. Fig. 1

_____ I'm learn - ing how to fly. _____

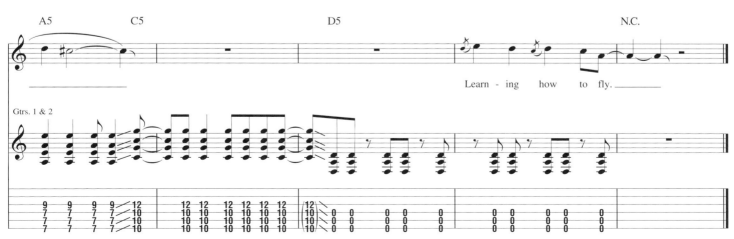

Learn - ing how to fly. _____

Gtrs. 1 & 2

Mistakes

Words and Music by Jon Micah Sumrall and Aaron Sprinkle

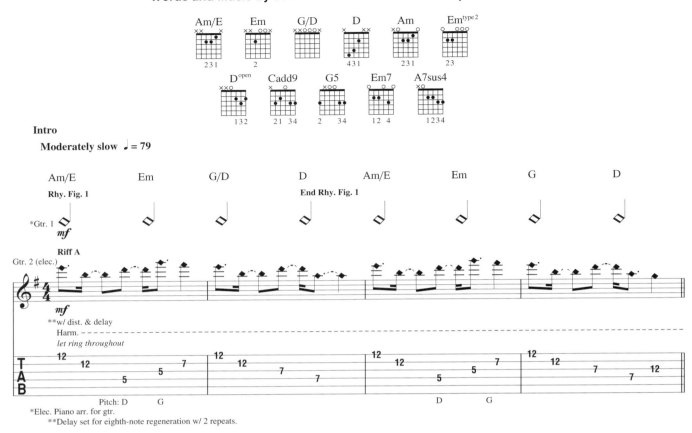

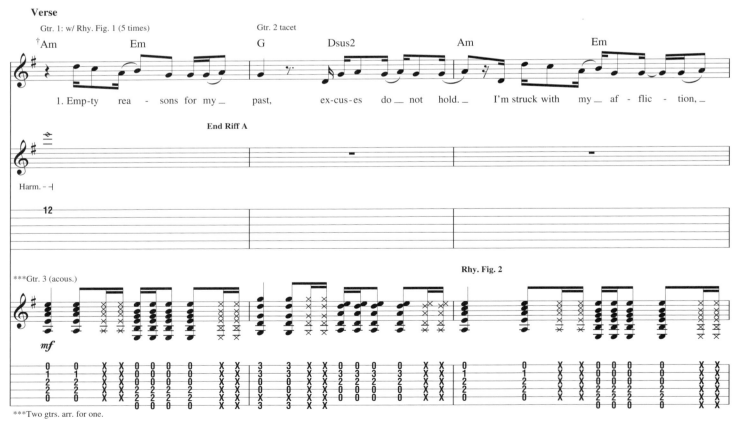

*Elec. Piano arr. for gtr.

**Delay set for eighth-note regeneration w/ 2 repeats.

***Two gtrs. arr. for one.

†Chord symbols reflect overall harmony.

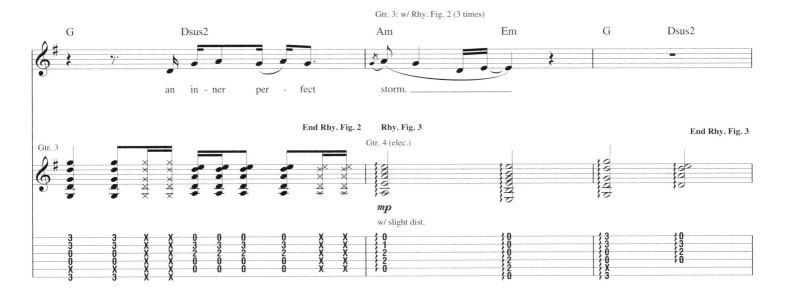

an in-ner per-fect storm.

Why did-n't some-one warn me to save me from my-self?

The pain is self in-flict-ed, the de-ci-sions were my

own. Now lis-ten to his-to-ry.

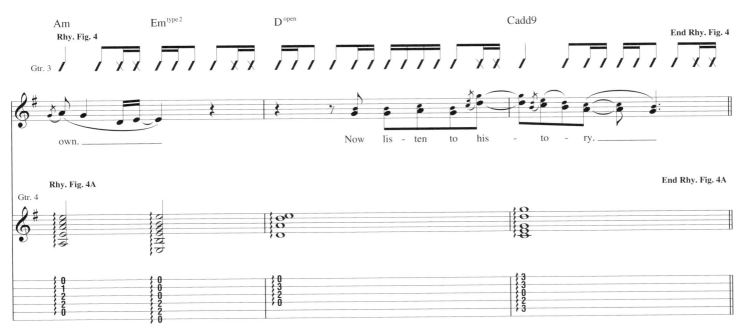

𝄋 Chorus

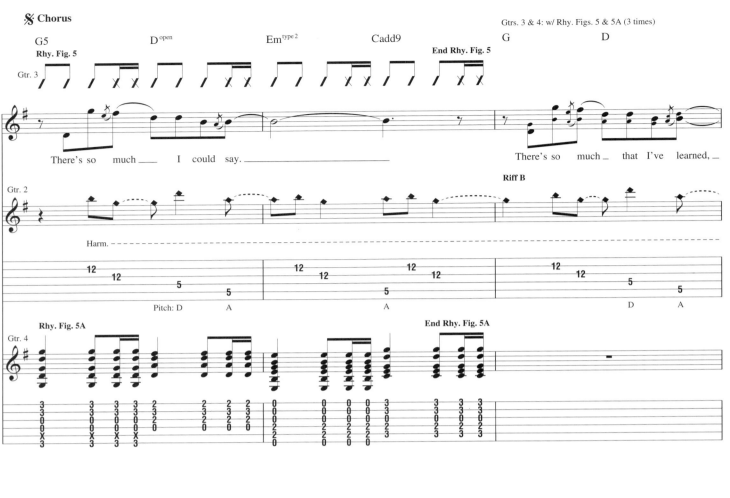

There's so much ___ I could say. _____ There's so much ___ that I've learned, ___

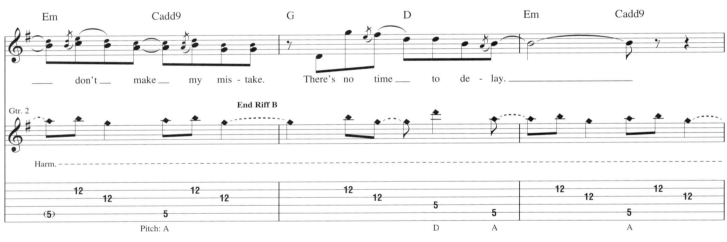

___ don't ___ make ___ my mis - take. There's no time ___ to de - lay.

To Coda ⊕

Gtr. 1: w/ Rhy. Fig. 1
Gtr. 3: w/Rhy. Fig. 2

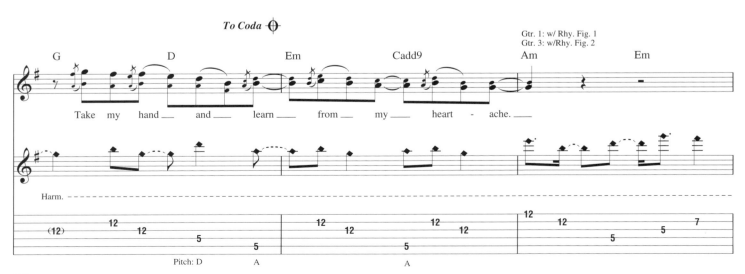

Take my hand ___ and ___ learn ___ from ___ my ___ heart - ache.

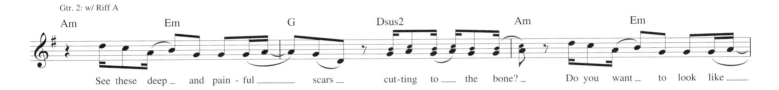

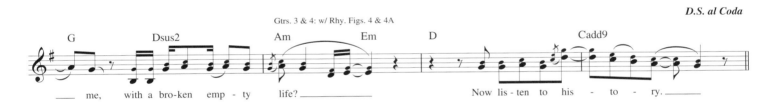

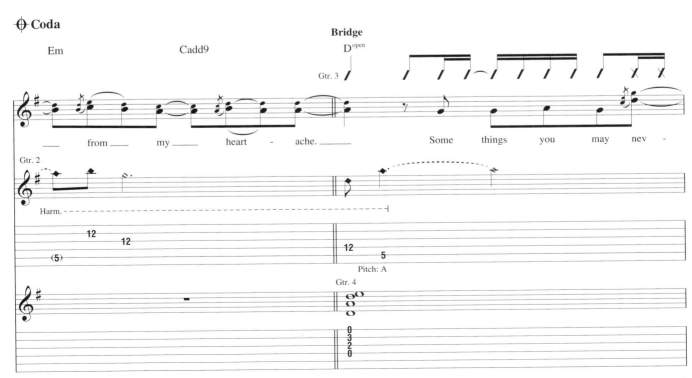

53

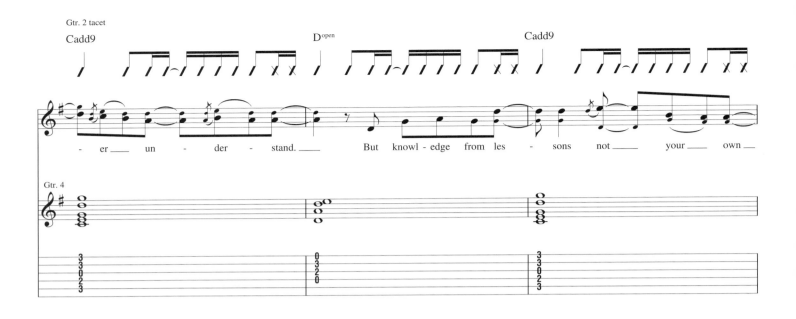

-er un - der - stand. But knowl - edge from les - sons not your own

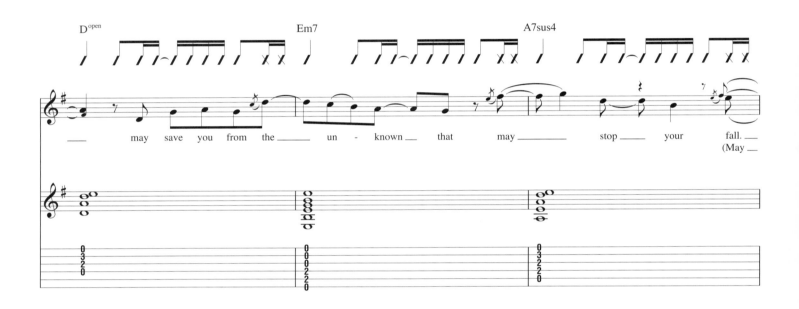

may save you from the un - known that may stop your fall. (May

Chorus

stop your fall.) There's so much I could say.

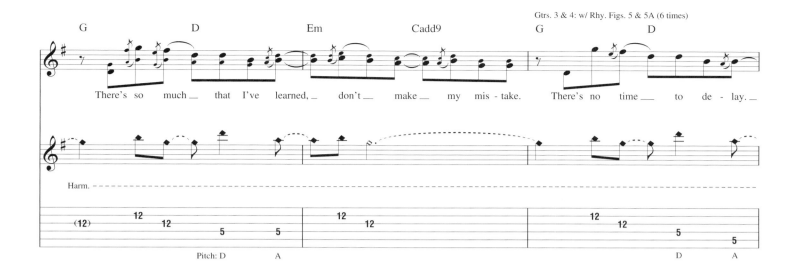

There's so much ___ that I've learned, ___ don't ___ make ___ my mis - take. There's no time ___ to de - lay. ___

Harm. -

Pitch: D   A   D   A

Gtr. 2: w/ Riff B (last meas.)   Gtr. 2: w/ Riff B (4 times)

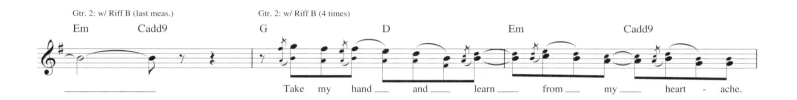

Take ___ my ___ hand ___ and ___ learn ___ from ___ my ___ heart - ache.

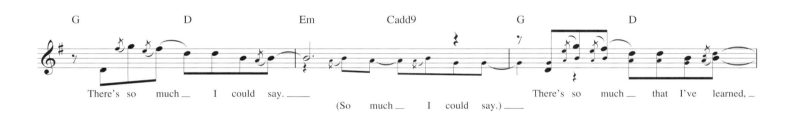

There's so much ___ I could say. ___   There's so much ___ that I've learned, ___
(So much ___ I could say.) ___

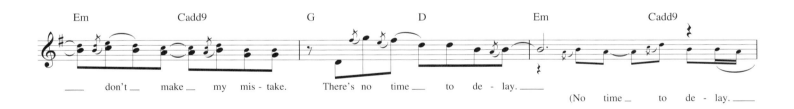

___ don't ___ make ___ my mis - take. There's no time ___ to de - lay. ___
(No time ___ to de - lay. ___

Gtrs.
3 & 4

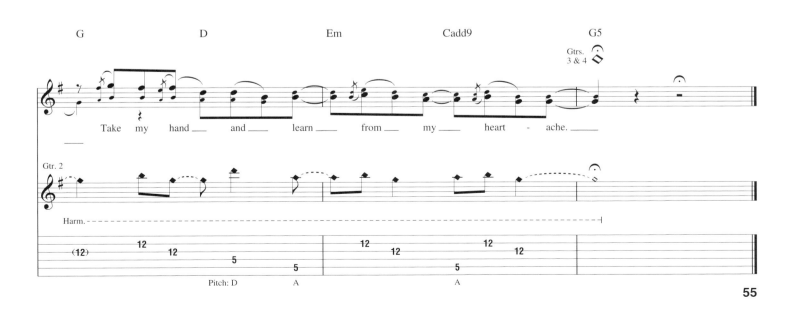

Take ___ my ___ hand ___ and ___ learn ___ from ___ my ___ heart - ache. ___

Gtr. 2

Harm. -

Pitch: D   A   A

Push Me Away

Words and Music by Jon Micah Sumrall and Aaron Sprinkle

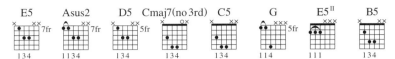

Drop D tuning, down 1/2 step:
(low to high) Db-Ab-Db-Gb-Bb-Eb

Intro

Moderately slow ♩ = 90

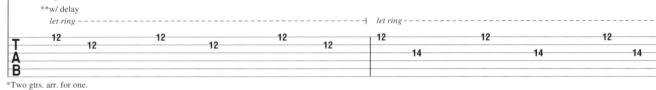

*Two gtrs. arr. for one.

**Set for eighth-note regeneration w/ 2 repeats.

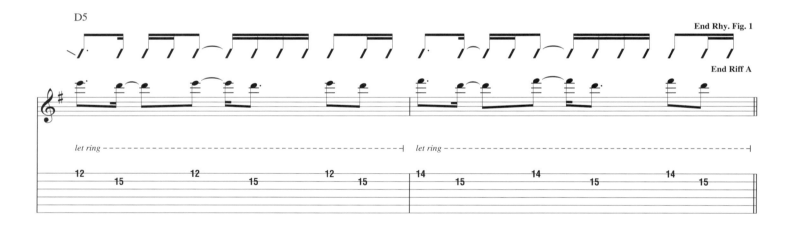

Verse

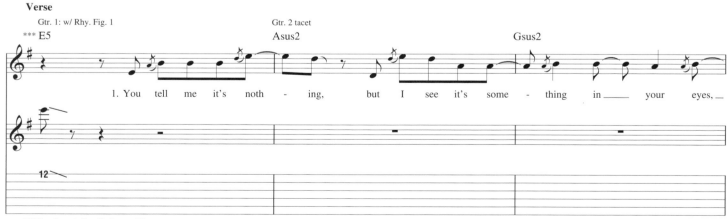

1. You tell me it's noth-ing, but I see it's some-thing in ____ your eyes, ____

***Chord symbols reflect overall harmony.

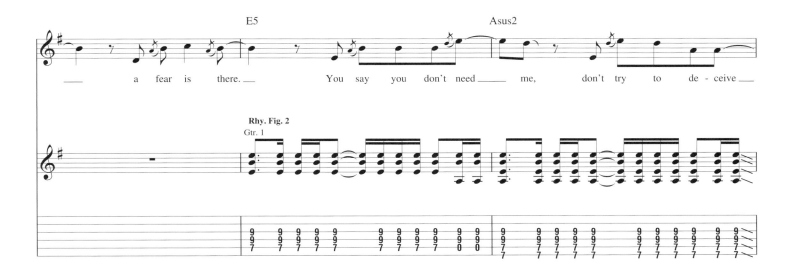

a fear is there.___ You say you don't need___ me, don't try to de - ceive___

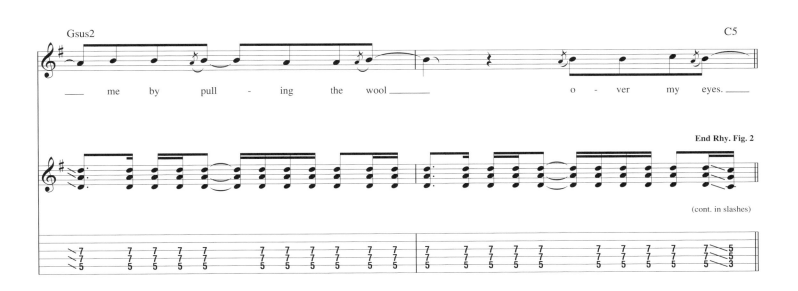

___ me by pull - ing the wool___ o - ver my eyes.___

Pre-Chorus

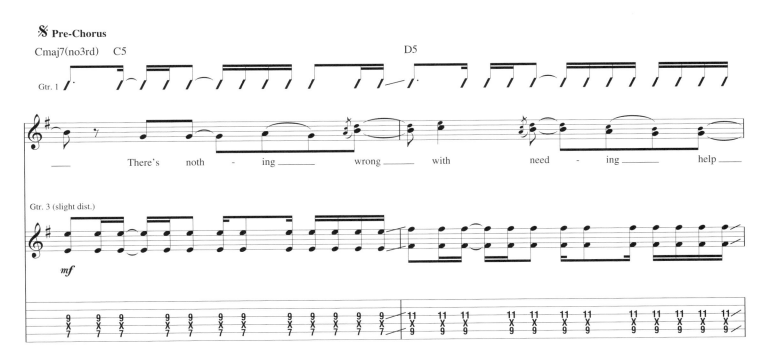

There's noth - ing___ wrong___ with need - ing___ help___

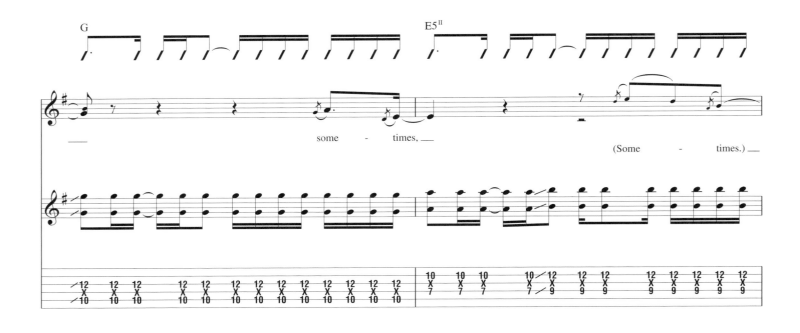

some - times, (Some - times.)

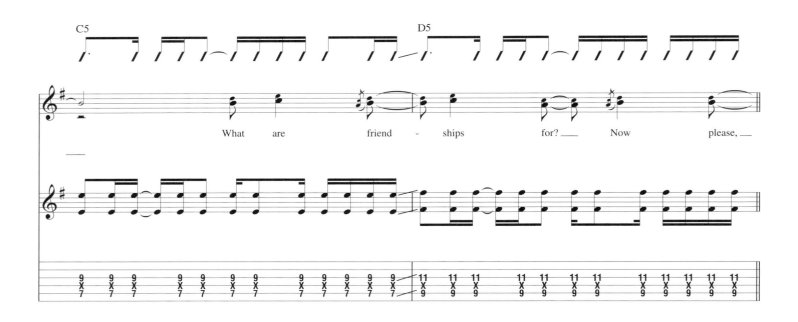

What are friend - ships for? Now please,

Chorus

Gtrs. 1 & 3 tacet

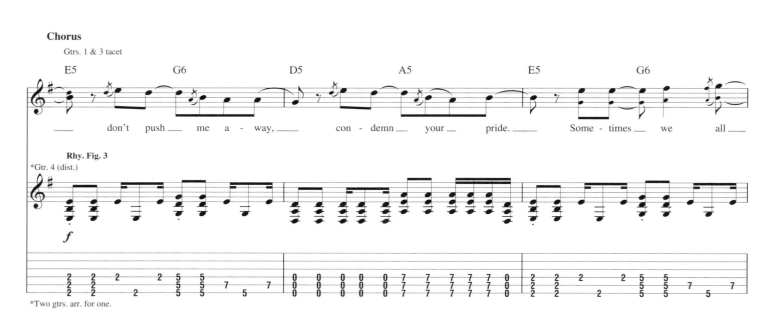

don't push me a - way, con - demn your pride. Some - times we all

Rhy. Fig. 3

*Gtr. 4 (dist.)

*Two gtrs. arr. for one.

— need a hand — to get by. Don't push — me a-way, — con-demn — your — pride. —

(cont. in slashes)

To Coda ⊕

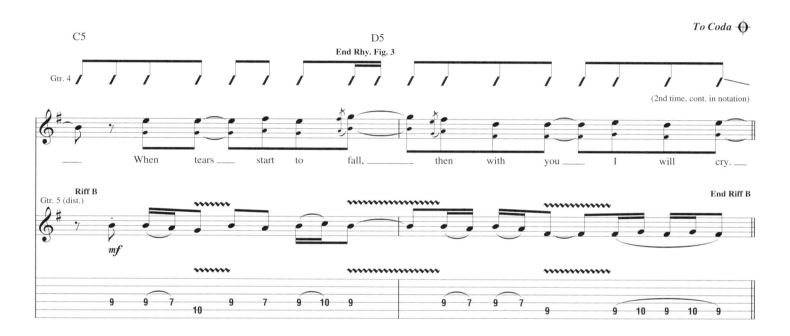

When tears — start to fall, then with you — I will — cry.

Verse

Gtr. 1: w/ Rhy. Fig. 1
Gtr. 2: w/ Riff A (2 times)
Gtrs. 4 & 5 tacet

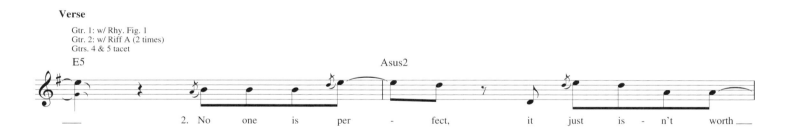

2. No one is per - fect, it just is - n't worth —

Gtr. 1: w/ Rhy. Fig. 2

— it to stand — on your own — though fear is there. — Don't be a - shamed —

D.S. al Coda

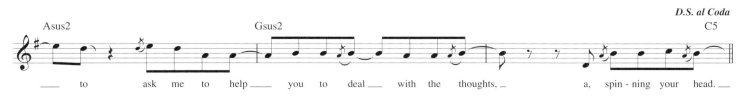

— to ask me to help — you to deal with the thoughts, — a, spin - ning your head.

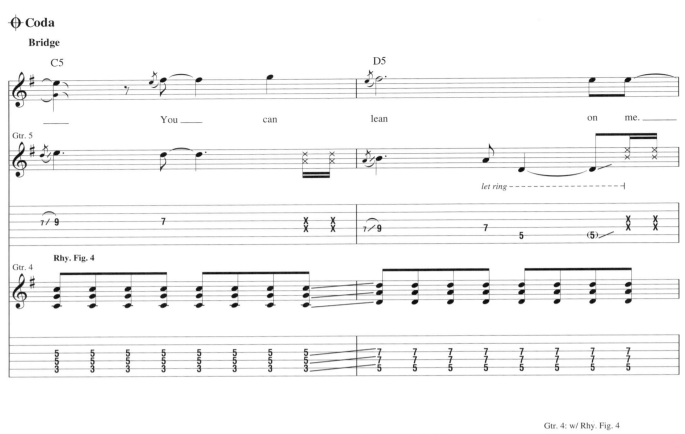

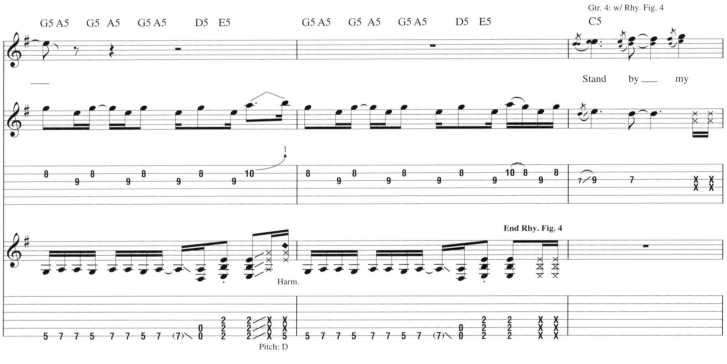

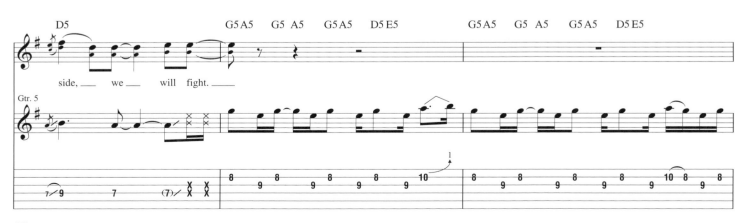

Changing World

Words and Music by Jon Micah Sumrall and Aaron Sprinkle

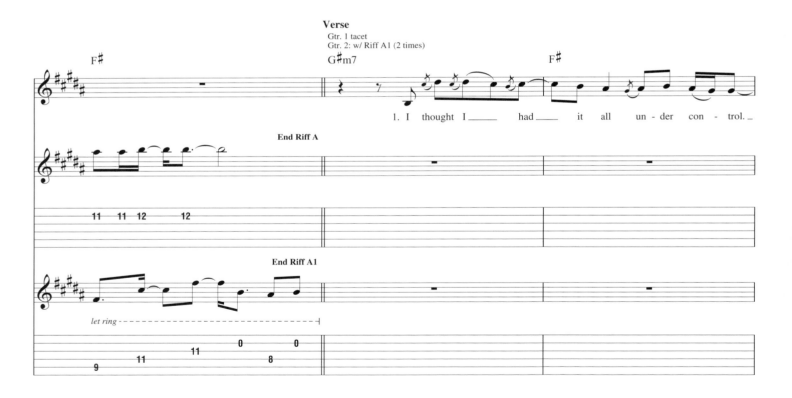

**Set for eighth-note regeneration w/ one repeat.
***Chord symbols reflect overall harmony.

were firm - ly ___ set ___ by the words that I say. ___ I for -

% Pre-Chorus

got how quick - ly things ___ can ___ change, ___ now my ___ vi - sion can - not be the same.

*Gtr. 3 (slight dist.)

*Doubled throughout

Chorus

Gtr. 3 tacet

My life ___ is ___ not ___ what I thought. ___

Rhy. Fig. 1A

**Gtr. 4 (dist.)

Rhy. Fig. 1

Gtr. 1

**Doubled throughout

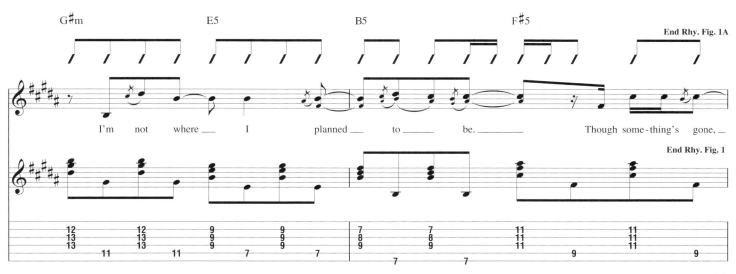

I'm not where ___ I planned ___ to ___ be. ___ Though some-thing's gone, ___

End Rhy. Fig. 1A

End Rhy. Fig. 1

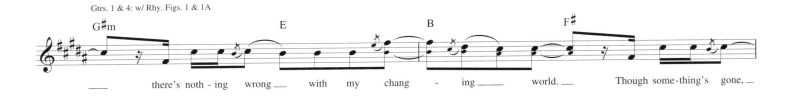

Gtrs. 1 & 4: w/ Rhy. Figs. 1 & 1A

there's noth-ing wrong ___ with my chang - ing ___ world. ___ Though some-thing's gone, ___

To Coda ⊕

there's noth-ing wrong ___ with my chang - ing ___ world, in my world. ___

Interlude

Gtrs. 1 & 2: w/ Riffs A & A1   Gtr. 4 tacet

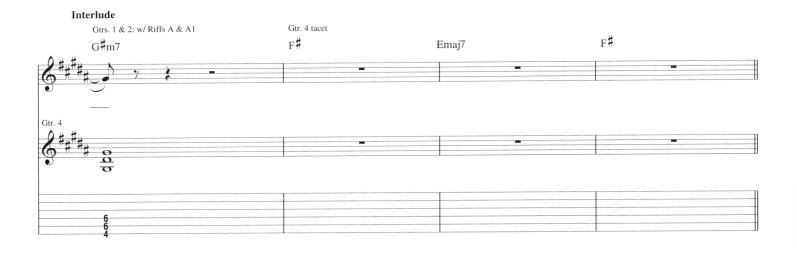

Verse

Gtr. 2: w/ Riff A1 (2 times)

2. I need to ___ let ___ go of my ___ des - ti - ny. ___ I need to ___ trust ___

Gtr. 1: w/ Riff A

___ in things ___ un - seen. ___ I be - lieve ___ in hav - ing faith, ___

D.S. al Coda

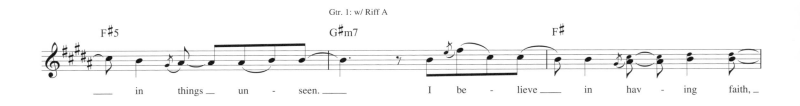

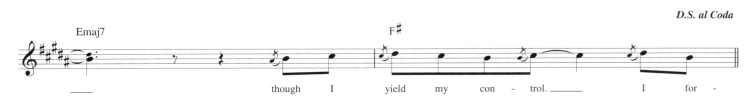

___ though I yield my con - trol. ___ I for -

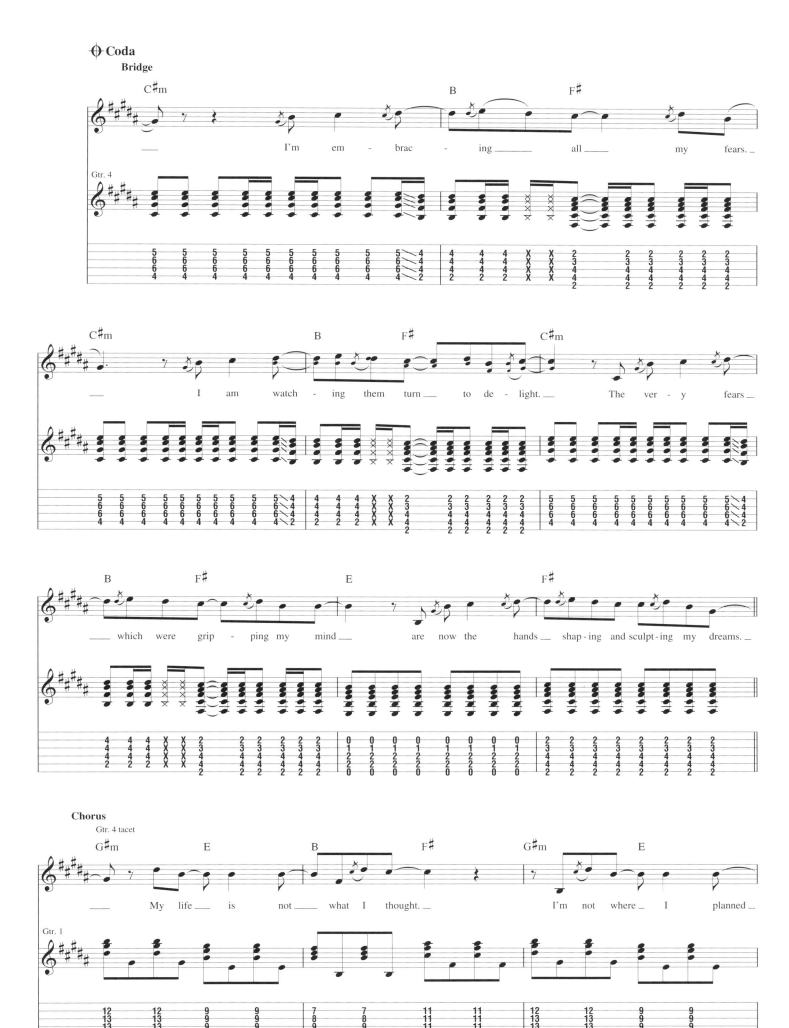

to be. Though some-thing's gone, there's noth-ing wrong with my chang-

-ing world. Though some-thing's gone, there's noth-ing wrong with my chang-

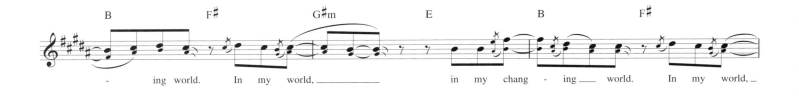

-ing world. In my world, in my chang - ing world. In my world,

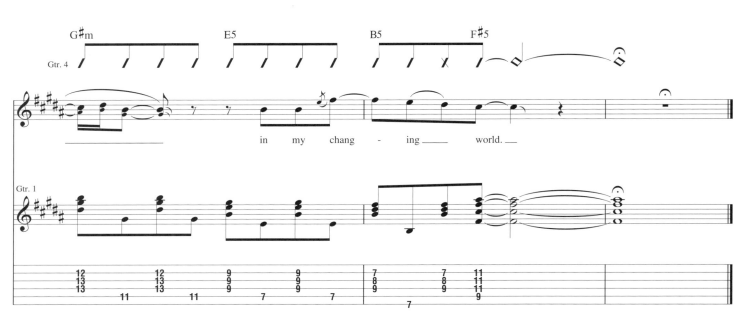

in my chang - ing world.

Million Dollar Man

Words and Music by Jon Micah Sumrall and Ryan Shrout

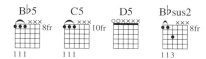

Drop D tuning:
(low to high) D-A-D-G-B-E

Intro
Moderately slow ♩ = 91

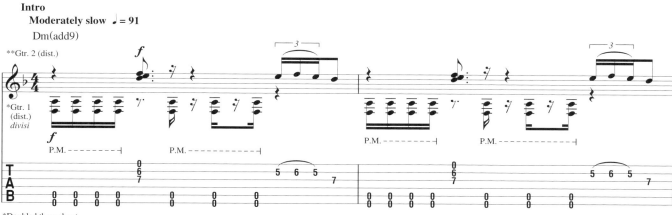

*Doubled throughout
**Doubled throughout

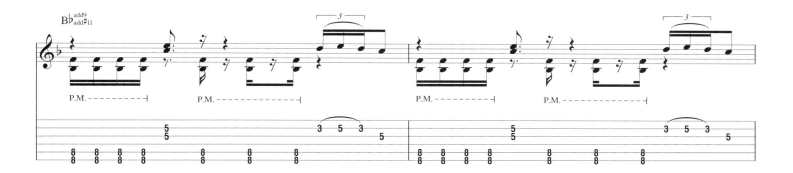

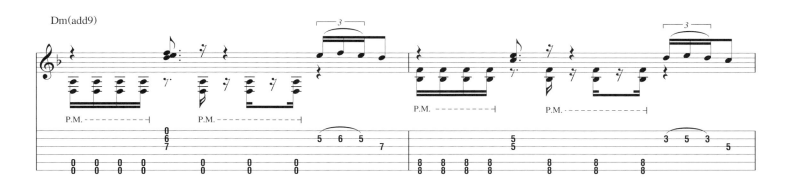

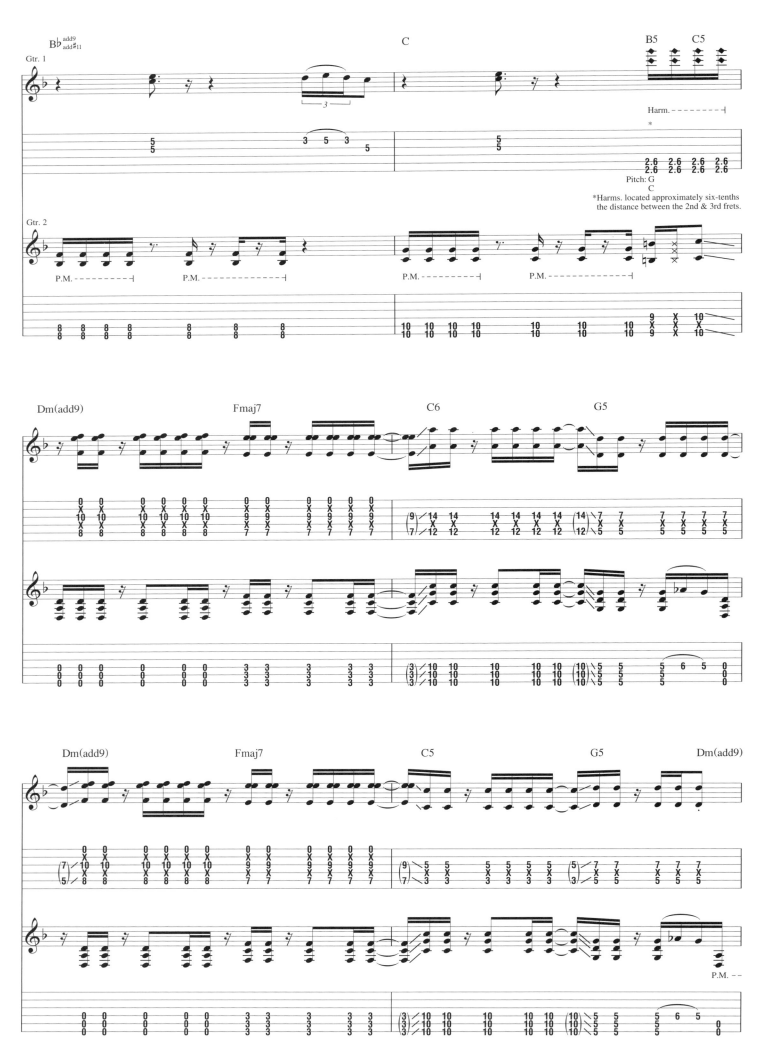

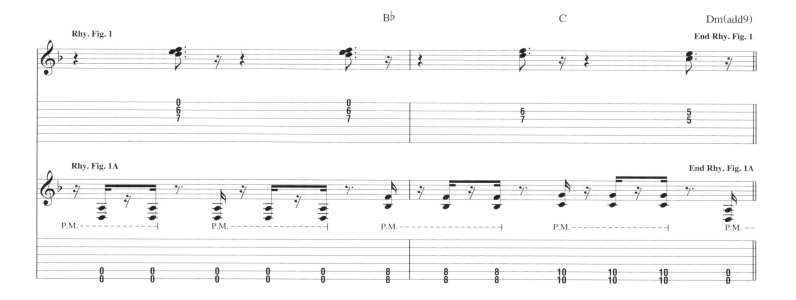

Verse

Gtrs. 1 & 2: w/ Rhy. Figs. 1 & 1A (2 times)

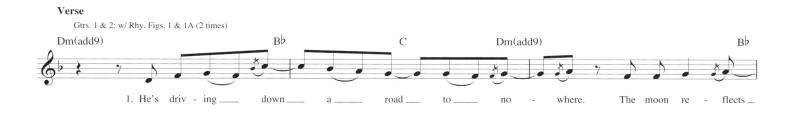

1. He's driv-ing ___ down ___ a ___ road ___ to ___ no - where. The moon re - flects ___

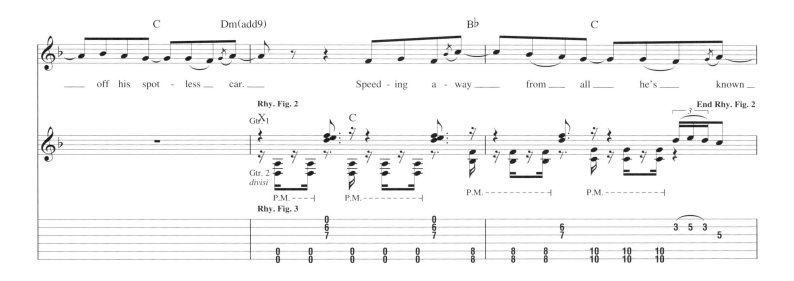

___ off his spot - less ___ car. ___ Speed-ing a - way ___ from ___ all ___ he's ___ known ___

Gtr. 1 tacet

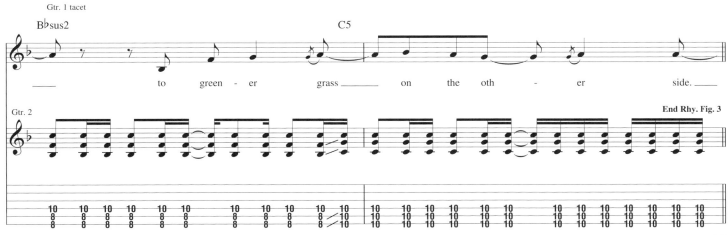

___ to green - er grass ___ on the oth - er side. ___

Chorus

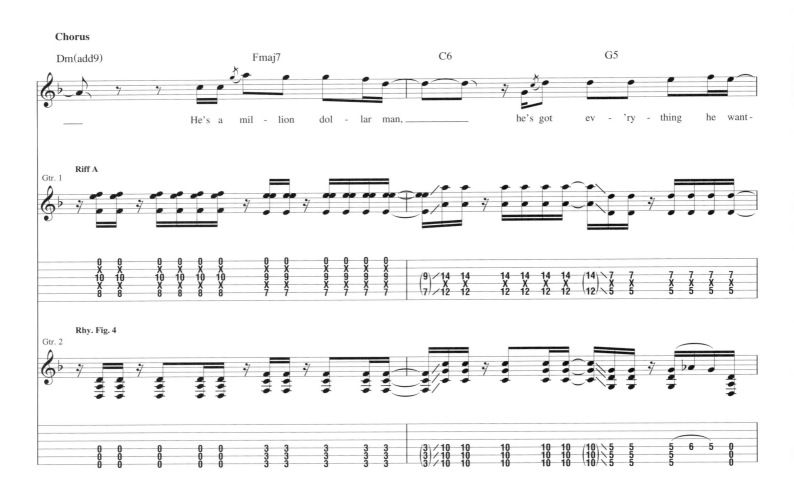

Dm(add9)   **Fmaj7**   **C6**   **G5**

He's a mil - lion dol - lar man, _____ he's got ev - 'ry - thing he want-

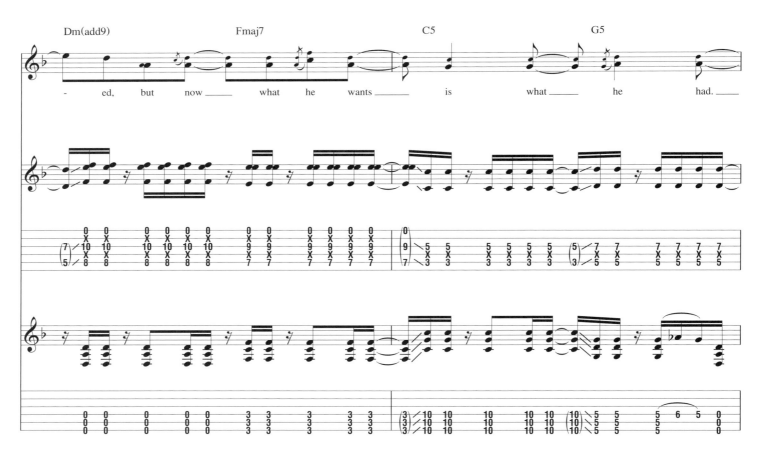

Dm(add9)   **Fmaj7**   **C5**   **G5**

- ed, but now _____ what he wants _____ is what _____ he had. _____

-less when you're a - lone, the grass is - n't green - er on this lone - ly side.

%. **Chorus**
Gtr. 1: w/ Riff A
Gtr. 2: w/ Rhy. Fig. 4

He's a mil - lion dol - lar man, he's got ev - 'ry - thing he want - ed, but now what he wants

2nd time, double-time feel **2nd time, end double-time feel**

is what he had. But he threw it all a - way for a life filled with cars

To Coda

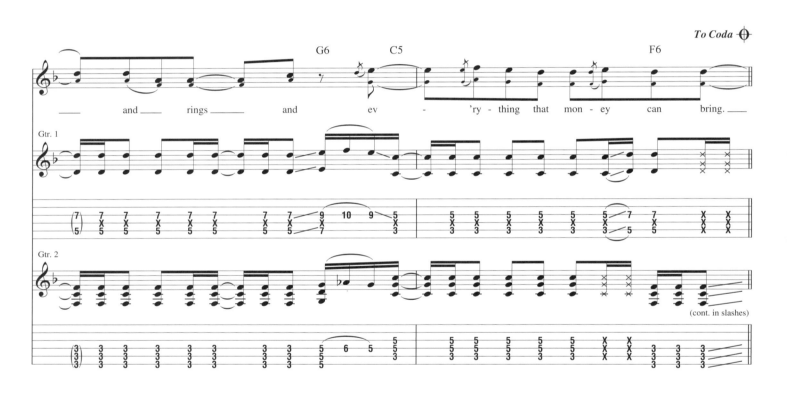
and rings and ev - 'ry - thing that mon - ey can bring.

Bridge

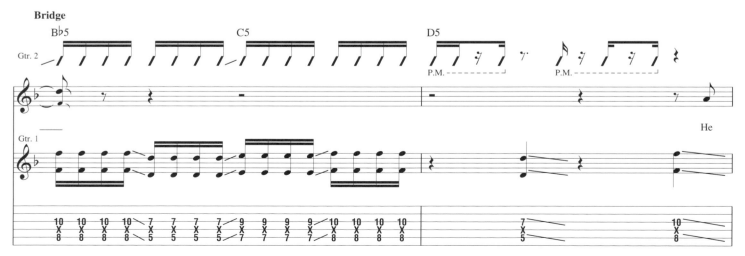

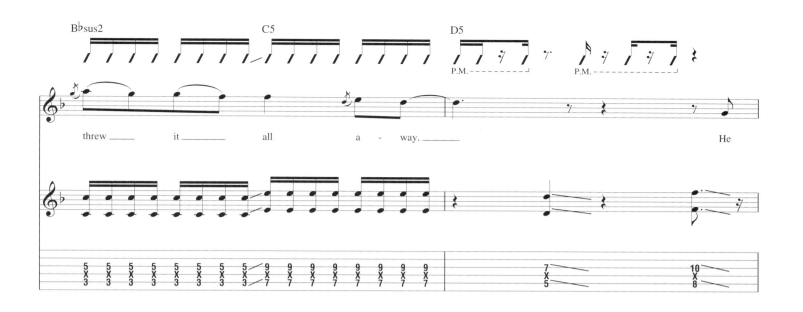

threw ____ it ____ all a - way. ____ He

D.S. al Coda

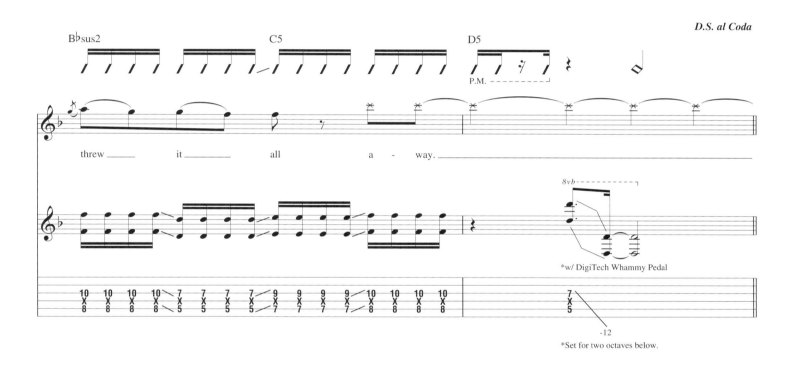

threw ____ it ____ all a - way. ____

*w/ DigiTech Whammy Pedal

*Set for two octaves below.

Coda
Outro

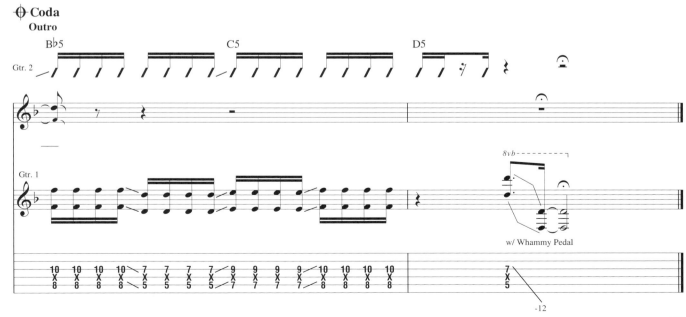

w/ Whammy Pedal

Legacy

Words and Music by Jon Micah Sumrall, Aaron Sprinkle and Ethan Luck

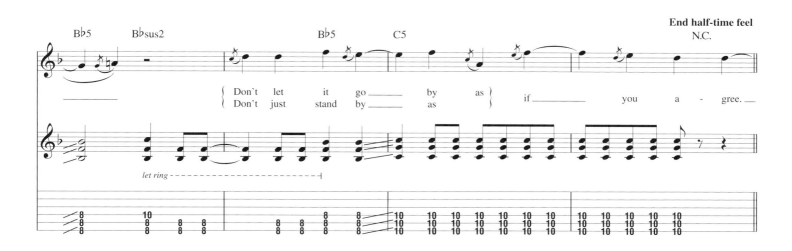

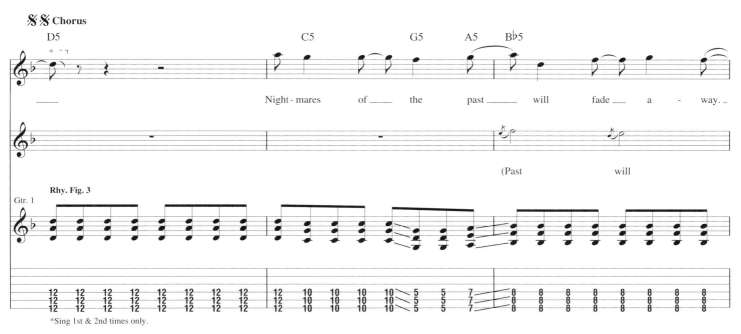

*Sing 1st & 2nd times only.

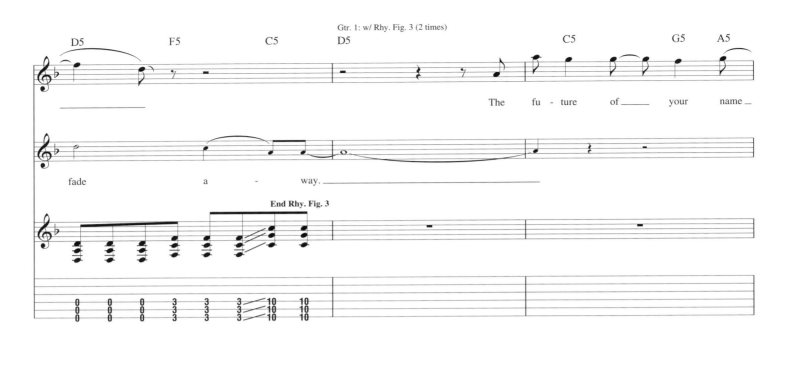

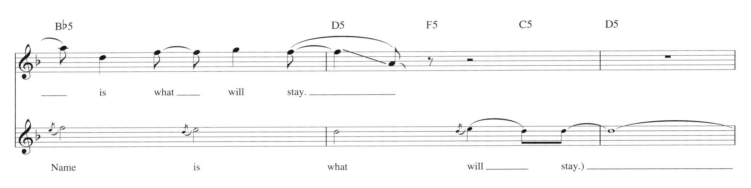

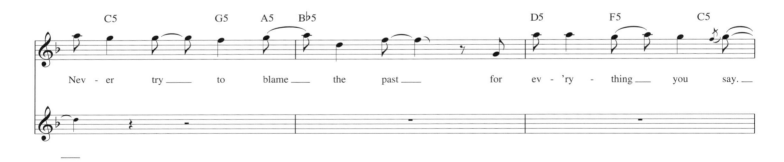

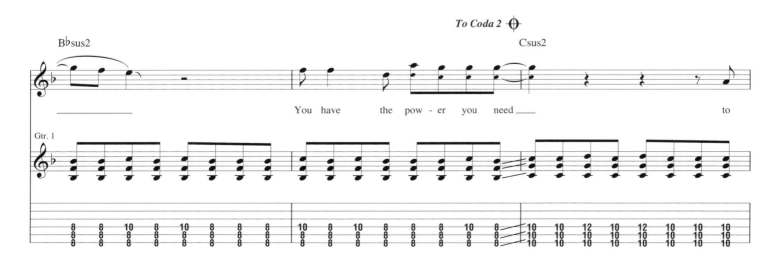

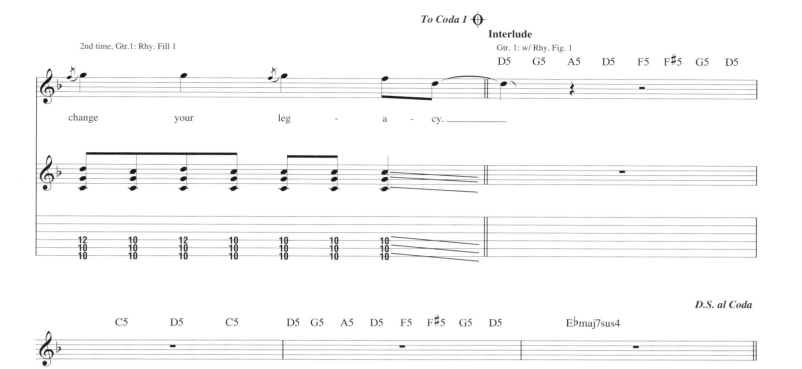

*Chord symbols reflect implied harmony.

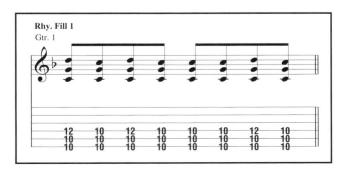

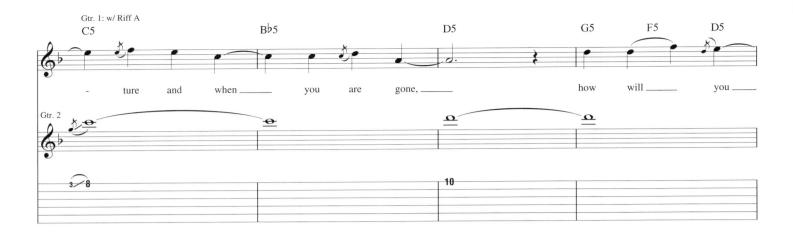

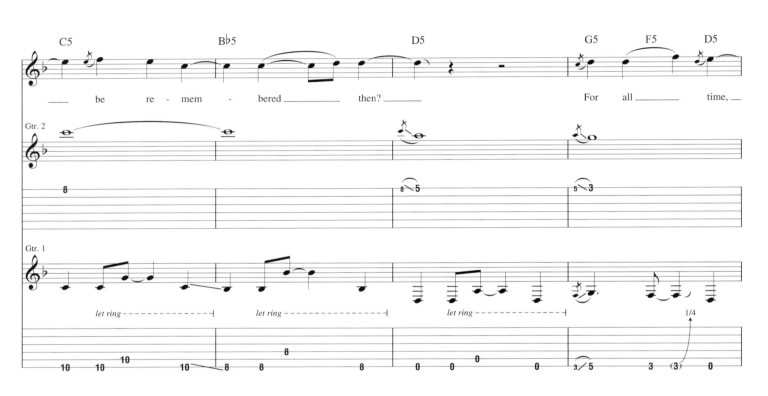

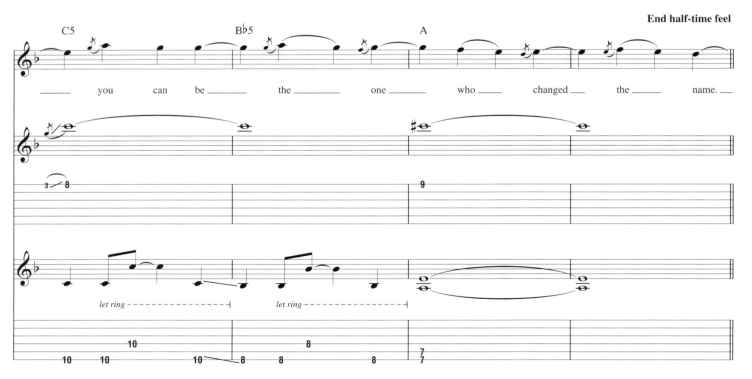

Interlude

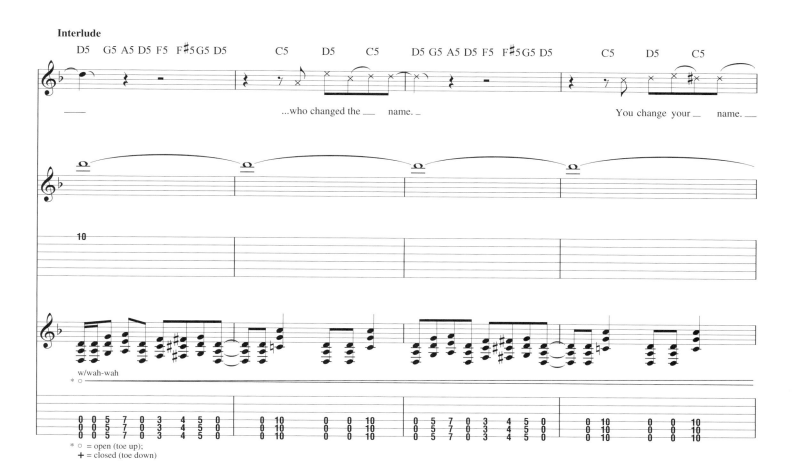

* ○ = open (toe up);
+ = closed (toe down)

D.S.S. al Coda 2

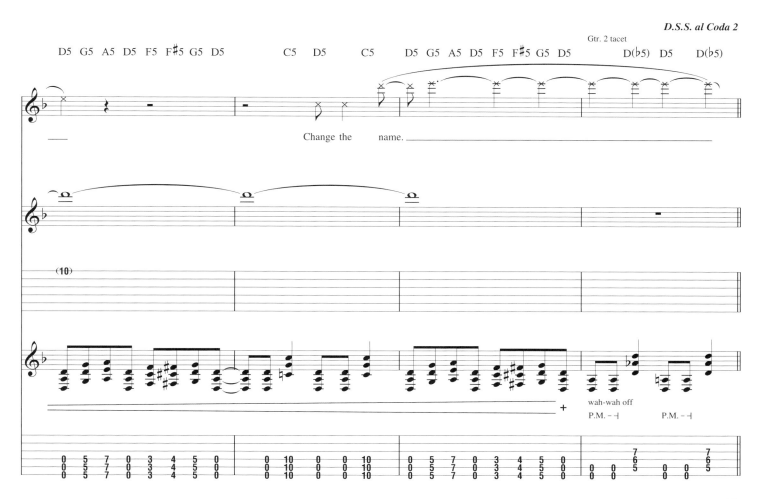